The Old Man

&

His Cat

Poems & Stories

From the Cabin

BY RODNEY DOMINIQUE

SPECIAL EDITING BY

CHLOE CUNHA

The Old Man and His Cat: Poems and Stories from
the Cabin

Printed in the United States of America, 2016

ISBN 978-1-945777-00-4

This book is dedicated to the past self. He had wants and desires but little courage & knowledge to pursue them. Give yourself time, past self, and pursue regardless of who's looking. You have courage, the knowledge will come.

This book is also dedicated to my parents and sister. My parents, Mommy and Pappy, instilled in me the creativity, sensitivity, and motivation that inhabit all Haitian people. My sister reminds me, without words, that I am loved.

I cannot forget to acknowledge my special contributing editor, Chloe Cunha. Whether she likes it or not, I owe much of the success of this book to her and her good eye. Unless it's not successful, then this is dedicated to a different Chloe. That's right, good old Chloe Gunha.

And to all of my friends that helped me be weird and appreciate the weirdness.

Contents

<u>Foreword</u>

Good whatever-time-of-day-it-is,

This book is a compilation of my Owner's writings over the past century and a half. After finding his various pages suffocating inside of a chest at the back of the cabin, I urged him to organize it to make space for other junk. He picked them up, went to the kitchen, and started perusing through them, muttering about the one time he was in a Cathedral or the other time he took a monkey along with him abroad. I took off to space out in the Day room and watch dust particles sway and dance against the afternoon sun. After many minutes, the sound of stapling snapped me back to reality. I rushed to the kitchen.

'I decided to put everything together in a book,' he said, fruitlessly stabbing 100 pages of words with a puny staple.

I asked, 'who do you think would read such a thing?'

He turned, saying he and I would, especially him since he won't remember much next year.

I guess at the end of all of this the benefit, dear reader, is exploring my Owner's mind, history, and having another nice looking poetry book on your coffee table. This would start useful conversations. Or, rather, end bad conversations by throwing the book violently to punctuate your frustration at your guest. Also, it will make my Owner happy. That would be good too.

Signed,

Thaddeus

Introduction

If you're reading this, congratulations, you got your hands on a sweet ass book.

As the front cover and title page already told you, this is a book of poetry and stories from an Old Man who currently resides with his Cat. The Old Man lives in a cabin in the woods away from the hustle and bustle of the City in order to collect his thoughts and live out his day's journaling the events that happen to him and his Cat.

The book itself is split off into 3 sections:

Section I: A Child at Home

Section II: A Gentleman Abroad

Section III: The Old Man and His Cat

The first 2 sections of the book are a chronicle of the Old Man's thoughts and emotions as he grew from a boy to a gentleman. As you'll soon read, the poems strewn about exhibit his emotional state and events in his life. He always wished to tell the truth slant in a bid to make events more interesting, but in time he learned to let playfulness take over with his words and phrases. The Cat will be providing clearer, hopefully helpful, asides. The last section is a collection of diary entries. He wrote to not forget things, as his mind is filled with past events.

You can approach this book in many ways. In fact, there are 9 official ways to go about it, if you follow the cycles below:

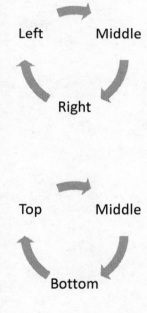

- From left to middle to right/top to middle to bottom
- From middle to right to left/top to middle to bottom

- From right to left to middle/top to middle to bottom
- From left to middle to right/middle to bottom to top
- From middle to right to left/middle to bottom to top
- From right to left to middle/middle to bottom to top
- From left to middle to right/bottom to middle to top
- From middle to right to left/ bottom to middle to top
- From right to left to middle/ bottom to middle to top

Without the cycles, there would be 3! * 3! or 36 combinations altogether.

- From left to middle to right/top to middle to bottom
- From middle to right to left/top to middle to bottom
- From right to left to middle/top to middle to bottom

- From left to middle to right/middle to bottom to top
- From middle to right to left/middle to bottom to top
- From right to left to middle/middle to bottom to top
- From left to middle to right/bottom to middle to top
- From middle to right to left/ bottom to middle to top
- From right to left to middle/ bottom to middle to top
- ...

Choose any route at your leisure.

x

SECTION I: A CHILD AT HOME

Cathedral[*]

At the Cathedral

The dew drops sit atop of the steeple

Resting amidst the sunset.

My enemy awaits at the front.

Those soft, miserable eyes follow my steps.

My mask hides my own soft, bitter eyes.

They don't need to be seen.

How forgiving I can be?

We'll begin our fight soon.

---

[*] Hello, this is the first footnote of the book. I'll try to be concise so as not to take away from the pieces. This poem describes the time my Owner and his friend were meeting for a final discussion. The details are murky but what I do know is they met, they spoke, they spited, and nothing was resolved. He returned to his wife at the time and could not get out of bed for a week. During this time, he watched a movie called *Ballad of the Fallen Angels* and wrote the poem during its more silent scene. It was the only form of expression that helped his grief.

3

The City

The hidden city, where magic lies, contains a profound secret.

A woman knows of those divine secrets.

She resides in affluence and bunks with both the good and evil of this reality.

They found their way from the reverie of the city's citizens. Both entities have reasons for being within: the good has affection; the evil has deference for her amoral skills.

Deception becomes tantalizing making her turn away from the good. But evil grows tired and his patience weary. He enters her gateway. The good gives chase towards a bright future.

In this realm no physical entities are permitted here. With the good and evil spirits wandering all time and space.

She lies in bed.

Waiting.

Settlement

My tears of joy become a waterfall of despair

My fears become reality and I transform into a boy.

I watch as people go by with haste and wonder.

If people are deathly afraid why scurry so quickly?

Your time can be for other things.

I tire.

I must go.

Paranoid or Paranoia

A dark presence within

Expanding

Burgeoning in every minute

Each breath drills fear to your lungs,

Your soul,

Your heart,

Weakens

Mind trembles, but soon the pain is all over.

He gains control

The Dark Prince returns.

On The Hill

Feeling sorrow within
I still find myself loving more

There is her, the girl strolling by, pigtails
scratching the wind
There is him, the boy marching heavily around
the ducks
There is her, the lady feeding the baby
There is him, the gentleman in suede looking
nonplussed
There is it, the bench the birds call their own
I want to show them all, everything

I cannot.

"I AM THE CHEESE"◀

Curse those who throw away soldiers for peace.

Pacifism can be achieved; destroying the lives of so many is repugnant.

Isn't the rush of battle exciting? A Suit says.

Becoming one with your machine and finally living up to your true purpose in life, a necessity we all need.

We create wars to settle disputes, the true goal is to conquer and proceed with life, whichever way we can.

We fight people for the people
We throw away our lives because of ethics and morals.

We become one with the people lost
We foresee our deaths and welcome the dreaded scythe.

We become the world's only weapon,

We are soldiers
We are human
Our emotions drive us to the brink of destruction

◀ I admit this is fully loaded. I brought this back to my Owner and he started babbling about the war he was in, the Titan War. He was on leave and had an abundance of energy & thoughts. His squad mates weren't the high-minded variety, so he wrote this during a fever blast and went back to war after hearing his comrades run. The title comes from a speech his commander gave:

"In this shit sandwich, politics and war are the shit, you're the bread, and I'm the cheese. We're the ones who make this shitty war eatable for the suits, our friends, and family back home."

8

Addiction

Watch me crumble below the depths of the earth, call upon me and see the horror created by you. Our lives revolve around the squalid threshold and sit upon it believing in an answer. The tears of life cannot provide wash forever; let not the drug control you.

Issues

Senses congested, $_{nd}^{mi}$ h ^{e} ^{c} $_{T}$ $_{I}$ c ,

Noises, smells, crowding my place,

People

Materializing

Without notice.

Fright,

Mischief teases my resolve:

DISTANCE

Meadow

The silent meadow watches the beasts lay to rest.

Dandelion spores twirl like helicopter blades

Softly landing on furry hides

With neither reason nor rhyme

The meadow watches and abides.

I imagine bees and butterflies, large mammoths of the wooly variety, scorpions, bears, and tortoises tending to their business, whether gruesome or not. The landscape takes it all in, letting them be. As nature should. It's also nighttime. That's what I imagine.

The Search

The four seasons advance swapping places, warning us of certain doom. Summer to Spring to Winter to Autumn. Clinging to the past I face fears ignored, wanting nothing but once was. I have to do this. Everywhere I look reminds me of how I was and how to go back. Everywhere there is fighting and mayhem that I cannot stop.

You came and stopped me. Not with the usual.

The sands of time fall in the hourglass and transport us toward our memories. Watching those memories are the hard parts of time. But ask yourself where does a memory begin and end? No one can start a memory, or end it; it takes emotions to begin "hellos" and "farewells".

Wandering, acquaintances tell of my travels. I fail to find a place worthy of me. The memories are vague. If any more clear, I wouldn't travel.

Spring to Winter. The snow covers tracks of love and clears away tranquility. You cannot stop me this time I must show my respects. But for old time's sake, let us have a waltz to signify what was once had.

Rowboat along the perimeter

Across the sea, a border separates our worlds.

We mosey along the border in our vessel.

It only holds two.

My weapon of choice is a machete,

For the battles ahead,

For the farming season,

As a warning to others.

My love carries mementos of her self.

A book of love languages,

A scythe to cut down redundancy

A brush to groom her life.

She carries sonnets her knapsack interpreting life with structure.

Having her beside me is a challenge. I am a mere word to the likes of her.

The Black Joker [note]

The battle rages on with no hint of stopping, two worlds collide with a flash bang of power.

I fight. I stop.

It wasn't real; none of what happened was true. I'm on the street with people staring, wondering why; I try to gather my senses until a sharp pain pierces the middle of my forehead. No one comes to help; they continue staring, remarking, judging.

A woman walks up. She's familiar yet has an unusual insignia on the back of her hand. Meeting my gaze, she speaks of the stars and life energy. The world blurs, the people disappear. I disappear but she brings me back with a passionate kiss. I resist but that titular life energy flew inside me.

A blinding light, such dark, ebony light, surrounds us. I shove her and wipe off the saliva. My disgust discharges from my eyes. She stands with tears staining her cheek like plum wine.

[note] I don't know how to dissect this. Was the boy dreaming? Who was the girl and how deranged was she that she kissed a stranger hallucinating in the street? His first reaction was appropriate. Be disgusted. This strange woman kissed you and you need mental help. What did she give you? I'm upset by this piece.

Without realizing, she died during that kiss. My own tears spill. A violet light shines on both of our hands. I realize now that she was much more; she gave me something very lovely.

Ionosphere

Floating

Wondering about everyone else

Are they waiting for me?

Seeing them laughing joyously

Wishing I could join in

But I float

Sobbing for a reason that escaped me long ago

Can she see my energy?

No matter.

I'll find myself and wander to other places

Vexed

This world of anxiety, such a pity

We walk, talk, and breathe, and believe in only ourselves.

It's hard to believe that we will receive nirvana from our "good" deeds.

We all deserve to be treated the way we live. All who believe they are better because they're stronger do not deserve to live.

(The boy stepped away from the manor window overlooking the farmlands that feed his life.)

End of the World[*]

The television's been on for some time, telling of current events. I barely listen as I chop onions in the kitchen. My attention is on my lost love, Faith.

"...And now the state of the meteor..."

A large chunk destroys the news station.

The knife drops and clangs with the floor. With my shortened time, I push past the sofa, dashed down the stairs and onto the street.

Calamity drove past not long ago.

I calm myself with logic, thinking of where she might be, routes to get there, etc... but on my way, I see love and peace filling the empty hearts of the citizens. Young lovers embraced and aged lovers relived fond memories.

Meteorites sprinkled on the town, pulverizing the stalwart architecture. Freckles of hope dotted my heart as I thought about her being alive, running

---

[*] My Owner told me that this came in a dream and the current piece is the best version. Typically, his dreams are premonitions or so he claims. This dream foresaw his divorce but he didn't read it well at time. It's hard to see things when you're focused on making something work, much like blindly running through an asteroid shower. I personally would have stayed at home and ate tuna and meatballs.

like I am to find me. My chest swelled with lovely motivation then.

Dazed, I continue the search. Through nooks and crannies, alleys and sideways, there was no neither luck nor sign.

Streams of lights flash as they curse our human existence. Some struck 10 miles away, others a mile. I don't care. I continue searching for her, the answer to my existence.

An hour of nothing later

I stop and sit on the curb, across from the Videomax where we rented our Friday night movies. Maybe I should give up on her. She doesn't love me anyway.

Our youth... The bent grass underneath us as the sun set over town. Our pinkies wrapped... The silliness of our first date worries one year before. This all rushes towards my mind.

Reinvigorated, I remember my cause. An act that qualifies as true love for my true love.

Soon I spot her, my one and only Faith. There she is standing with eyes full of hope and the sweet fragrance of laughter and joy emanating from her. The dark sky and ruby, red fire surrounding us bring out the azure blues in her eyes.

But who is he?

The final shower strikes.

Antagonistic Symbiosis

Ever growing and teeming with life, the creatures go off and perform their duties.

The pale sky watches as they attempt to revitalize the Earth.

The people gather oozing with glee.

The creatures notice the benevolent anarchy before returning to their duties.

Browned grounds turn to Green landscapes as the hours go by.

The people settle into their groups, picking up the Greens for adornments, necklaces, hats, and bracelets, and underwear.

The creatures can't and won't become these people. They will labor and make anew until the people leave.

That's some Dream...

I'm falling and I don't why.

How far am I from the ground?

I guess I shouldn't do anything, that's what someone is telling me.

I don't know what to do? Nothing is stopping me.

The fall helps in realizing how things work and why they exist,

But the epiphany starts to fade and I am dumbfounded once more.

The stars appear to fill below.

I feel energy draping over my body, rolling away from my center to the extremities then bouncing off my fingertips.

It is released, elating me

But I'm still falling and I don't know why.

An Essay on the Trials of Love

Love throughout time has been acknowledged as a powerful emotion capable of changing a human's characteristics. However, throughout time this has also been transformed into a complicated term since love can be associated with many things. Its uses vary from time to time and cause confusion to those who have only witnessed love or have never heard of it. Though this is extremely rare it is possible for one to have never heard of it. For some people, love is received at first sight meaning when one is born the mother/father immediately holds him/her and swells with mixed feelings of pride, affection. No one knows why this event occurs repeatedly but apparently, no one cares.

Love has the ability to dissect itself into subdivisions that creates instead of a simple liking for things. When love is not returned however, it can cause deep hatred and jealousy for others that receive love with grace. Love is a mystery though, even to those who receive it. In order to figure out or even solve the entire aspect of love one with enough interpretive skills and who is somewhat unaffected by it can investigate it and complete it.

Downtown at Noon, near the old Jayman's Store Outlet [a]

A boy has brought himself into the crossfire and uttered these words:

"Tis ashamed that the people I met have been fooled for a small period of their lives by a jester. They were unable to see the lines separating the mask and my true face. Every time I am shown, one has a feeling of total self-approval rush over them due to my fatal flaws. But I only have these flaws due to my inability for self-control in an excited state. The only way for me to ever give absolute intelligence is to be in a depressed/sad state of mind or blinded with anger/rage. This is silly, yes, but who is to say humans are not silly, for, unbelievably, I am human; even though I lack any highly developed social skills and mating skills. But since humans are stubborn and arrogant, at times I shall withdraw my status of being a homo sapien and become a new creature that is below average

---

[a] I read this piece many times... I'm still trying to remember the scenario that spurred the emotions in it as it was explained to me. Why a clown? Assuming he was even human to begin with. Maybe he was a primate with emotional issues or maybe an alien who got tired of being here? I'm having fun trying to figure this out. I recommend doing the same, dear reader.

when compared. Luckily, I pulled this stunt for over a decade and realized my kind does not belong here. So I step into a barrage of screaming bullets, not to save a female who is but of a score years but to rid myself and witness other creatures in different galaxies and record data. Thank you for listening."

The boy's whereabouts have not been confirmed but many say they can see a black-cloaked man sitting on a meadow near the country looking towards the sky.

Ten Little Gatekeepers

Ten little gatekeepers play in the sand,

Earl went to fetch water; be back soon,

Nine little gatekeepers play in the sand,

Penny is counting quarters; be back soon,

Eight little gatekeepers play in the sand,

Jacob and Josh are playing freeze tag; be back soon,

Six little gatekeepers play in the sand,

Ida is mystifying the sand worm; be back soon,

Five little gatekeepers play in the sand,

Con Con is signaling the skies; be back soon,

Four little gatekeepers play in the sand,

Piper found treasure; be back soon,

Three little gatekeepers play in the sand,

Amy found the cool blue; be back soon,

Two little gatekeepers play in the sand,

Executor wanders off; be back soon,

One little gatekeeper plays in the sand,

Chaunice sneaks up from behind; be back soon,

No more gatekeepers in the sand,

I guess the gates are open.

It's raining, Goro... [*]

A meadow...standing beside it
A few feet away, a girl.
Standing closer was my reflection
       Listening

Her name escapes me but
She is special
She spoke of elegance
       Of love
              Of smiles.
She spoke of laughter
       Of joy
              Of songs.

I remember these instances; strangely.

Her toothy grin and haughty laugh
Rippled the meadow
Crescent waves spread out
She hasn't stopped talking

I don't care
I smile, I'm happy.

She smiles and laughs...again.

I...no, the reflection loves her.

---

[*] The significance of this piece, according to my Owner, comes from the two characters...I think. Or perhaps it's due to the forgetfulness of the narrator? I can't recall well and my Owner is out right now so no real explanation will be given. The scene does evoke a sort of out of body experience. A man seeing his past or other dimensional self and having trouble feeling the other's situation. That proverbial other is in the meadow's reflection, worlds away but so near. I think this explanation is different than the real meaning but I like it all the same.

28

I don't know what I feel.

She stepped closer.
    She held me. She likes me.

    I guess I'm happy
    I held her
    Gave her a peck on the forehead

Now it's raining
The reflection blinks
    Wiggles

Go, Go, Cactus Man

The carpet was made especially for guests; it is plush underneath my feet. The children usually sit around it. Their dolls living inside the world of the carpet, telling life stories with humor and pathos along the way. I sit, rocking, and listen, blowing bubbles in the air knowing they will pop somewhere. Humph. My wand is not working correctly. This carpet feels so soft underneath my feet. Oh, I feel the rhythm the children create on the carpet. There is the girl I like, no wait there she goes. What could I say to grab her attention? A bug crawls on the rug; I will leave it alone. Wow, those children have energy but they don't use it wisely. I would like to play too.

The Real Folk Blues

The days are getting shorter around here

Waking up expecting to be something

Becoming something else entirely

Becoming tired, condescending

Before bed

Before dozing off to names of friends long gone

You whisper good tidings to yourself

The real folk blues.

'Diary'

It was quite a bad day today; I found everyone and everything hostile, rude, and unnecessary. I've decided not to do anything else.

Day 1:

I decided to live one more day; I cannot die without going to school for the last time.

9:00 am

Another one of my classmates is spilling out shit again. I am glad I won't be here.

12:22 pm

Something changed my decision to living for another week. Figuring it was my last day I decided to actually show my emotions and I found out more about my friend than I would have if I were to talk in my usual tone. Staying alive for another week won't be so bad...Especially if this keeps up.

3:00 pm

After I got home and after lying on my bed, my mother came home and expressed her love through her usual way. After dinner, I decided to stay alive for another month. What's one month compared to fifty years?

Day 2

I've decided to stay alive for a month. It won't take long.

11:10 am

Class seemed interesting; of course, I'm using a monotone voice. I want to get into a fight so badly the feeling is unbearable. I'll just punch someone and see what happens.

5:55 pm

Two fights, two wins, two groups jumping me soon this week. Losers. I don't see the reason why a group of people needs to hurt one person. It may possibly be for moral support. I'll just grab a bat, and butterfly knife. Smash and Cut.

Day 25

I haven't written an entry in so long. It's due to my studies.

1:25 pm

I received a good mark on my report card for history. Didn't expect that. The day is coming up and nothing has altered my decision just yet.

7:10 pm

No one's home and I am listening to music. Everything is serene and lovely. Especially since the song is a good one. My senses are focused all on the song. If only I had more time to do it.

Speak Like a Child

Prancing around the villa

Pillars reaching the sky

I wondered if the day would stay like this forever.

My strides were large,

As large as I can make them

My grin, five feet wide.

                    Eighty-five years.

I'm not surprised.

My strides are ten times bigger

My grin five times smaller.

The villa is more of a shack

The pillars barely reach the top of the trees.

Intoxicated, I wonder

What would have happened if I stopped frolicking about and stay?

I think I was able to run faster back then.

Once those clouds were purple and green

Now they're barely taking form.

I made no documentation of my youth.

I thought it would last forever

Or at least time would stand still...

Cowboy Funk

Riding at the speed of sound upon my trusty, sturdy steed, I race towards the setting sun that is destiny.

At least that is what I would be doing if it were a western.

I am the thief, the most wanted. I am the bounty.

I give chase on the streets of Gadhelic, protecting myself from hunters of all shapes and sizes and races. A punch here, kick there, a few bullets whizzing by. I elude with unorthodox, Eastern beats and fighting techniques. The hunters jump into the cockpits of their ships hoping to gather the forty mil on my head.

In the old days, the sheer thrill was good enough for any cowboy; they aren't real cowboys. Just punks looking for loot.

Now if I were a bounty hunter I'd have some real old school fun.

Viaggio

After a hectic day, I can finally rest...But I
cannot stop thinking about that woman; it's been
plaguing me since a week ago. The compassion I feel
is quite draining.

I was in Italy for vacation, you know just to clear
my head, not expecting anything to happen on a
Monday. I guess us walking on that street in that
moment was a small jest of God. She ran like raging
bull, knocking every single coffee table in her wake.
My eyes were cast down, counting the tiles on the
street when a great force slammed me down and a
woman staring at me, frightened. Her hair was
short, black and she had sweet, green eyes filled
with pulsing stars from my head injury.

She pulled me up, profusely apologizing. After
we settled the whole incident, I found that her name
was Olivia and she was running from debt collectors.
What she owed, no idea. A few more apologies later,
she walked me back to the hotel room. I kept
insisting that she needn't follow me but she kept
following me, asking about my head. She stated she
needed a place to stay, saying that she wasn't safe
anywhere but with me.

Why did she say that, why with me is she safe?

It seemed weird to have a woman, as beautiful as her, to find safety around me. I'm a weak man. After an hour and a half of her hiding in my hotel room, I decided it was time for her to leave. Not to be mean but I felt as if she wasn't right for me. I started to sneak her out of the hotel since she was an uninvited guest to begin with. We went towards the back exit of the hotel out into the alley. She thanked me for keeping her safe and kissed me on the lips. I felt warm for a little bit. Once she went out onto the street bullets began to fly. Her body tossed around, twisting in the ballistic wind. She spilled on the street. It was a queasy sight for any pure of heart. Gut pieces oozed into the waterways under the street. Her disconnected right hand looked as though it was crawling to safety.

I cried. She didn't deserve it.

Later, I learned she owed $328,069,058.94. Once they were done, I went back to my room and drifted to sleep hoping those men do not come after me.

In the Study with the Piano

Somebody play me that memory

I def don't know how it goes

It's sad, sweet, and I knew it complete

When I wore the under man's clothes.

To this day, I know not of frolic, of taffies, or even
peaceful naps. I sit in solemn silence counting the
lies I've told with the cat on my lap playing chess
and thinking strategic. I want to be the master of
the universe but then I would know, but who does
know, except the numerous many?

Sing me a song, piano man,

Tonight the mood is just right,

I feel like grooving and shaking my fears away

Bringing the lost memories to life.

In the Land Of Twilight...

You do not kiss me with your eyes closed anymore. Now you see me every moment of our love session. I remember those past moments vaguely. They were luscious moments. Like the phases of the setting moon your eyes went and you envisioned the man of tomorrow at that second. I was stalwart, cunning, witty, a jester, a father, a foolish boy, a mature man, the magician and the knight.

Now you see **ME**.

That ain't kosher. I want you to see the dream that I wished to life rather than the mistake you made. I'll close my eyes for you.

I see you. You have no fault. That is why I chose you...I hope the rain seeps into your eyes, blurring your vision so the illusion continues on.

Friday *

I have gazed upon the eyes of medusa, I have stared into the fathomless soul of the Id, I have glared into the pond of true reflection and yet I have never looked at what I have looked at on Friday ever before.

---

* This is one of the few selections that is succinct and doesn't fiddle faddle with jazzy prose. I would say to shorten the paragraphs a bit. Anyhow, I'll take this space to for another type of musing: my own story. Earlier today, a strange figure entered the home. It was our neighbor, Pablo, wearing his suit of pearl and brass lapel sitting on the left side of his suit. He asked if my Owner was home, not bothering to knock or even call, mind you. I told him he was out for his 50 mile stroll so he won't be back for some time. Pablo sighed, with a bit of panic escaping with his frustration. He informed me that his rooster, Amuro, and Amuro's wife, Endive, needed help. The wife was experiencing birth complications and needed another set of hands. I offered to help but Pablo informed me that my claws might get in the way. Endive's cries carried over from the roost. I grabbed my winter mittens and went to help anyway.

We saw Amuro sitting in front, despondent, his head flitting to and fro with each cry from Endive. She was rocking back and forth, bloated and straining for relief. Pablo picked her up. Her tiny chicken legs kicked the air. We could see two eggs crowding the way out. He held her steady while I lightly pawed the egg on the left back inside. She wasn't cooperating with the pain. A few moments of pawing and an egg shot out then another. Amuro peaked inside and wailed with joy.

They named the eggs Dolores and Katherine. Amuro already picked out their future aspirations: Dolores will be a musician and Katherine will be a carpenter. Endive rolled her eyes and got comfortable with her two eggs underneath. She quickly reminded Amuro that this was just step one of the parenting process. They need to hatch before either of them can play the guitar.

I don't apologize for this aside. As on that Friday I experienced the screams, goop, and smell of the miracle we all know too well.

I have touched the burning magma of a dragon's belly; I have held the softest material only created for slumber, I have gripped the coldest snow that would have frost bitten many a man and yet I have never touched what I have touched on Friday ever before.

I have tasted the bountiful fruits of Eden, I have licked the honey of the comb, I have devoured the most horrid foods and yet I have never tasted what I have tasted on Friday ever before.

I have heard the cry of the banshees, I have heard the screams of children, I have heard the intoxicating melodies of sirens and yet I have never heard what I have heard on Friday ever before.

I have smelled the sweet perfume of marmalade, I have sniffed out the most putrid of tracks, I have smelled the stench of pure hatred and war and yet I have never smelled what I have smelled on Friday ever before.

What an experience.

You were lovely that day.

I want that sensation forever.

My love, my dreams...and you!

Against the post I stand and stare,

At the tree reaching the sky without care,

My legs are feeble and cold like this post,

I insist I see the Holy Ghost.

Weighing in every spectrum gram by gram,

Calculating all that I am,

Factoring in every flaw and sad moment,

Subtracting all happiness that has been lent,

Differentiating the final difference.

Ground control to the major in the sky

With his head held high,

Sitting here eight days a week.

I wonder where the contact will be held?

I receive no notification from the highest council,

To be the best that I can be.

A war of roses is concluded by the cunning of a dandelion,

Thwarting the best to reach his grave by choice.

She had a dream to beat them all, to have the world become pacifists.

To end the world in such a way is suicide or genocide of the Id,

A confusing vortex has led me to this supersonic speed,

Heading towards my proper displacement.

This old chess set is played two different ways by a bay and father.

The winner plays the best and shows their skills.

In a flash careening to that past, I see the rook travel diagonally,

In wonderment to the black square.

That vortex opens showing three entities of three identities.

Midnight Carnival

The room explodes and their faces burn.

Now his blood is on your hands. There is little time for a second chance. Now paint your face with blood and tears. Smear it on with a page from the good book that no one reads with a misspelled word that no one knows.

Enter through despite the patience and turn around for a secret that we do not wish to share.

Pray for the old and place me where we used to kiss.

Your heart, it's getting smaller. Was your defeat disheartening?

NO! A puppy sits now on the tar. It's quite the same if your mind began hemorrhaging. Cannot wait for the sunrise and waste my time with your embrace. Someday someone's going to look at me; there's no time to waste.

"Pushing the Sky with a Gaze of Blue"

I arrived...

There were five people in the mansion. I greeted them and waited. My attire consisted of a dark jacket, grey button down, suede shoes, and a tie. I took a quick glance at the stairwell wondering if the coming scene will be surreal. My ears caught her footsteps; my eyes widened only a little when her body emerged from the top of the stairs. My presents for her: a potion granting the drinker prolonged life, and a specially picked weed to guard its keeper. There was no place for it on her gown. Her outfit was a pink dress, two slits running at the sides from her knee to the end of her shin. She had on leather boots. Simply stunning. Goodbyes were exchanged and we entered the chariot, or a red station wagon, if you wished. A smile here, and a smile there; no words could be said to liven the moment.

We arrived...

With date in hand, my entrance emphasized by my temporary cockiness. She giggled at the sight of my walk. That did not last long. The cathedral was lively. No one wanted the night to end. We searched for our comrades among the parade of one-day tuxes and puffy sleeved gowns. We sat to chat with them walking out moments later for merriment. So we made our own merriment.

We danced...

The room was dimly lit to fool the people into romance. Quite a plan, or scheme whichever it was. A quadrangular floor was our setting; the music was the plot, the people the characters, and I the narrator. We tangoed. At first there was distance then I summed up my courage and pulled her close to me, I choose not to describe her soft skin in great detail. The dancing started and skipped. There was so much to do: dance, kiss, meet each other's gaze, kiss, and touch, grope, run out back, out the door to the station wagon, drive to an empty house, to each other, inside each other. Instead, I sat, and stared not knowing where to start. She was disappointed. My desperateness went to its peak; I rested my head on her shoulder. How juvenile. I must have been equivalent to a pitiful puppy. Time needed to pass quickly. My clothes did not make the man.

We waited...

The dancers annoyed me; they were gay and festive, on the prelude to a holy day. It would be

amusing to play this scene backwards then my
evening would be delightful. As the night ended so
did my dreams and her patience. We walked back to
the chariot fully realizing nothing happened. She
looked away to the stars until her mansion was
interrupted her sight. She approached her door. I
stumbled out of the car to complete the drop off
ritual. For a moment, I saw delicate beauty then I
cried. I was no man. She went inside for slumber. I
went to my homestead for deep reflection.

I hope she forgives me.

Training Day

Fighting caliber high,

The sword that forges a legend creates the hero.

In the depths of reflection,

Lies the buried past of deserted memories.

Watched over by the gods of war,

The young warriors ingest their victories to feel its full effect.

Hordes of towns and villages brought into the crossfire of dynasties.

Myth becomes truth,

Truth becomes legend,

Legend makes a hero,

Heroes create history.

Dream #13

I concocted this dream two fortnights ago...

I dreamt of swordsmen finding the ultimate treasure and living their dreams in luxury and adventure. It was a boring dream. Luckily, it was only that night. It resembled that of the make your own adventure books, which I loath to no end. I urinated things more interesting. I found the breakfast joyous. It took my mind off the dream for a while. Coffee, a cigarette, and tuna melt help remedy any situation. The breakfast itself wasn't what took my mind off that nuisance of a dream. The decision I had to make was what did it. Should I have the cigarette or the sandwich first, once I make that decision should I then have my coffee? Alternatively, another bite/smoke? It took me a long time to decide. I preferred this life than that of the swordsmen. They used every ounce of energy trying to find royalties I would have rather wandered the earth in search of...I don't know. That seems more virtuous then an abundance of riches; it's also sickening for unworthy people to have riches, damn actors.

I remember the decision I made earlier this morning. I had the tuna melt first then some coffee

and lastly a cigarette. I went in order of sensation.
When a progression is made, in a particular order,
things make sense. I believe I went to my closet next
because I was excited that day for some reason.
There was one pair of pantaloons left. Already I had
my shirt on since I wore it the night before. My
plans for that day were to spend some time with my
old, by old I mean senior citizen, girlfriend. She calls
me her little 'Prufrock'. I grew a white 'wizard' beard
to see and hear what she would think. I picked up
some oranges from my grocer along the way. I cut
my nails to look sharp and now I'm regretting it.
Luckily, I brought my Swiss army knife along so I
could have my midmorning orange snack. What
would be my weapon of choice? Am I close range or
far range? In my younger days I would make a good
warrior. I was tall, clean haircut, sharp vision, well
built, fast, and a sharp wit. How far would I travel
and what I would do with all that time? Maybe
strain my brain over what I would have for lunch. I
was never able to make up my mind on small
decisions. I walked through the park wondering
where we were going to meet and remembered. It
was in the park. No wonder. My body remembers
more than my mind does. Sitting on this bench

reminds me how I waited for her in the past; now that I think about it, I should've had coffee first. As I was hanging a clock in my bathroom, I slipped and bumped my head on the sink. As I lay there, I had a sudden revelation, a bizarre and absurd thought of my own mortality. Was this body truly my own? Have I lived? Was there some sort of place for me? If purgatory existed, was I already there?

It was good fall weather; the leaves were a nice color of orange and brown and the cool midday breeze felt oh so right. 'I'm bloated like a mongoose and I feel right.' What time was I supposed to be here? Was it mid-17th century or four O'clock? If I remember correctly she told me sometime between 8 a.m. and 8 p.m. That was remarkably specific...I think. A young couple passed by a while ago. They were gorgeous holding hands and kissing. It reminded me how stupid I was, but she never minded it. She wore black for many occasions and was barefoot. I still cannot remember when I'm supposed to be here and when she left. There is just the fallen leaves and myself. It is 6:13 I haven't seen her yet. I could go through time faster if I practice my sword attacks and thrusts.

She finally arrived; I heard her sandals from a distance.

Dandy Lions (I)

Fireflies illuminated the field with no grass blade left in the dark. Demons from every species gazed upon it with wonder and delight. The fireflies were not the only thing that gathered the fleet of monsters. The stench of blood was in the air. The demons sat in circles admiring the caravan of lights for miles. Nightmares walked towards the great field to view the festivities.

Days prior a civil war took place. Factions sprung from the depths of human cruelty. Alliances formed from jealousy. The only way of stopping was to end the lives with hatred. Four armies, four ideals collided on this playing field with no remorse for the defeated. Many wished for peace, to end the struggling, but humans cannot go on living without battles. By believing, that peace cannot be acquired without war led them astray from nature and straight into the battlefield. With every soldier's

---

My Owner wanted to speak on his experience in two ways. He couldn't decide before on which to keep, so he expressed it twice. I rather like the longer piece as it expresses the demons not otherworldly, like a satanic demon, but rather as another creature simply created. It also fleshes out the humans though I would say it's rather one sided on their temperament. I don't blame him for such a view though.

morale at its apex, the war began and ended within a fortnight.

As the warm summer sun roasted the rotting carcasses of the dead soldiers, their spirits rose in hundreds of directions to spirit world. No one can say whether their souls entered nirvana or a terrifying nightmare but it was apparent that many did not wish to go. The afterlife was an experience of the end, they had more to do. With their hearts riddled with anger, each body combusts. Bursting with fury installed from the war. The smell of melting flesh attracted one demon; she stood there looking upon the flames, the aroma of dying human souls filled her lungs. That is what kept her there. Others followed suit.

Now demonic spirits from far and wide bared witness on the circle of life. They were not only addicted to the stench, they wanted to see what happened to these mortals after death. What type of hell did they inhabit, what joy occupies their heaven? Do they possess the same God or worship one at all?

Dandy Lions (II)

The glowing field.

Fireflies hover and skip over the blades

As Demons examine

Whispering wonder and delight to one another.

Spirits of hate

Stench of blood

The allure permeates the air

Gathering the monstrous fleet.

While the Nightmares fascinate

The summer moon regards the rotting carcasses.

The dying souls

Fill their lungs

With a meditative high

One Ice Cube at a Time...

The lips, the teeth, the tip of the tongue receive a blast of cold from the solutions of the world. Synchronize the joy of it all to your guilt.

A seemingly unsolvable cube emerges with magnificence from the depths of the world and tries no more. The freeze numbs and offers a momentary salvation for all.

Then the spring sets in.

Three periods for people suffering.

The next phase consists of blinding pain with artificial coolers in grails to leave enough room in our brains for thought. I am given pain throughout by forces. To solve these daily problems I am given a temporary solution. I call them solution cubes.

Tales of the C-class Warrior

I strive, I fight, I lose, and I improve, while I bleed. What else could be said but that I am inferior to higher ranks and superior to lower ranks? I have the will to fight.

SECTION II: A GENTLEMAN ABROAD

The T Ride[a]

Shall I find retribution for every sin I committed this midnight? The old woman sitting over there, has she done anything wrong tonight? Will her life fall unto my shoulders and rely on my judgment? What about the boy beside her? I hate children, but still what of his existence? Will he go through the pain and joys of many a woman in order to suit his need? I hate children, but I cannot bear to see his charred flesh on the railing. Can't the conductor let them off first, I don't care, I want them off.

The passing lights flow backwards faster and faster, the reflections of the reverse train leading the way to paradise. Is it because of me that this car is going to an abyss of nightmarish visions?! What was it that I have done wrong, is it irreversible, was it a chain reaction leading towards this moment?! How bad shall the fire burn, is there even oxygen in such a place? I will escape from such a realm you are bringing me, Conductor, and I will see to it your ass is eviscerated! The lives on this train are my responsibility now, I chose my fate. No god can

---

[a] This is the mania felt after deciding to leave for abroad. Simply put, he was traveling and the event of the War seeped through his mental barriers that usually block out unwanted thoughts and emotions.

control it! I exchanged my last token to take this and to realize my folly.

On the other hand, is the folly even mine? Who has chosen to erase lives on this midnight carnival? Was it you boy, the same kid who hasn't even licked the sour balls of life yet or you old hag? Your solemn sitting doesn't fool my mind! I haven't the nighttime to deal with your liking.

Why the sudden darkness?

Are you evil enough, Conductor, to lead innocent lives to Beelzebub's tomb, or is it because you have a grudge? Perhaps revenge or deep-seated issues motivates your clockwork? A mother or father leaving you, maybe it was a lover that tickled your fancy then stole and shattered your heart that made you take such a profession.

Grates! Remember, grates exist! Every quarter mile, the surface people will hear the telltale screams of the passengers. There's proof of your villainy.

I have not the foggiest for why I decided this train. Was I tired of walking? Is walking a sort of repentance? I haven't figured out why I'm here yet;

do not take that knowledge away from me! We passed the Lechmere Station and given farewell to the Red Line. The scum of these Gotham streets, I hear their pain and moans, the vicious smell of dried urine on their beards, stained with the blasphemy passed down generation after genera—How much longer is this train ride, you fantastic villain, you?

How fast are we traveling and how long will this pain last? Is this car my final ride, is this hell altogether? How many people shall die tonight? I do not feel well enough to die. Don't tell me that I am the only sacrifice. If I am to go out in a fiery blaze of glory then I MUST HAVE COMPANY! If a man dies alone than for what reason would his soul travel to another plane? There is no one amongst it, so it has the choice of lingering. Heaven and hell are for companies not individuals. Therefore, we shall die together.

Wonderful, I can go to the depths of hell knowing people will burn for their own sins and to participate in my party.

My wife, my wife has not appeared yet, can I at the least change my outer garments to be presentable at death.

There is only one stop left, and I have two to go, until final damnation. The lights have caused numerous passengers seizures not to mention a clear dislike for your engineering skills. I for one am getting tired of all of this; my boredom is sapping the very focus I placed upon your wicked villainy.

I hear sirens screaming in agony. Finally we are here. I can see where I am going; some sort of paradise considered by those fueled with guilt and in need of justice. Is it this place, is this where I am to go? Oh wait, hold on. I know where I am.

The Castle [a]

With the east side of the castle facing me, I sat at the bar reading my usual spy novelette. Between the castle and the bar window I gazed through, drunks wandered the street, making no mischief fortunately. To my left acquaintances from various skirmishes, to my right the intellectuals that played war games with our lives. I felt little connection to them. As my acquaintances sat, I read. One would call it strange to not offer a single salutation or even a glance to people I know. I believe it to be ordinary, blatantly ordinary. How so? Well, my aloof polite disposition. I chose not to disturb their groove. They were having a laughs and pint. The acquaintances & intellectuals performed for each other. Two thumbs down. Any ordinary human would simply say, 'Hello friends, how is the day/night treating you?' Then take it from there.

Not I.

I had the temperament of individuality, to keep to myself. Reading my novelette sparks my enthusiasm. I conversed with myself.

---

[a] His war buddies came into the bar. That's all that he would tell me.

66

There's activity outside now.

Now, the night is old; the elderly walk the sidewalks as sprightly as children do. Disturbing. The lights inside the castle flicker. I see movement, an abrupt, staccato rhythm. A silhouette fills the window frame with contempt and fear. Then it happens. Resolve. I narrow my focus. The silhouette blinks in and out of frame then disappears. The light bulb burns out, finally at rest.

My acquaintances played childish pranks on each other. I felt a foreboding towards them. They immediately dismissed my statements on the castle. The intellectuals, a few moments ago, departed.

I do not look in the mirror of my drink. As I would agree with the people's opinion. A rumpled, milt skinned punk talks of misdeeds? Rubbish. For the time being, until I look out again, I adopt the look of ignorance and believe in the dream.

The acquaintances possibly believed me to be their friend. I did not grant people such a title so easily. Until I find them worthy, they shall keep the title of acquaintance.

Until I have more evidence, the silhouette is guilty. The figures outside the window are gone and the night ages. The light is still off. Only the slight wind pushes along now.

Now the acquaintances are gone. One of them gave me a pat on the back and farewells were exchanged. I sat at the window looking at my spy novelette again, thinking what led them to me. They, possibly, may not be my friends. It may be possible that some cosmic force decided our partnership, not our personalities or one's attractions. As probable as that may be. I shall expand on this further in my chapters. I returned to my novelette since I got to the good part.

Simply Put Math = Beauty

A complex plain consisting of numbers 1 through k,

Radiates our givens to an exuberant degree.

No land, whether point or space, presents such

A sine of grace as a function of waves.

We can power ourselves up and define the

Magnificent proof of our next value.

Root us and find the basic core.

E us and make us natural.

Graph the pattern and discover what it means

To exist beyond the real, the reality.

Our alphabet is centuries dead

And still proficient.

My Owner wanted to have fun for old time's sake. So, he went to his first love: mathematics. He went to a 3 continent wide festival away from the city. I've heard of it before. I went with some buddies back in my University days. Rainbow ticker tapes rains from the sky all across the festival with all forms of people vitalized with good cheer. When you're on the train traveling throughout it's like going through another dimension. This is how he experienced it.

Dimensions rift, characterizing the

Fundamental history of our youth;

The prime years.

Those days that integrated the volume of our fun,

Evaluating the mass of our fantasies,

Were the stepping-stones of great discoveries,

Of bedazzlement in a splendiferous field.

We aim for the median in our arguments,

Causing modes of betrayal.

Forcefully pushing a derivative towards the edge.

Vector meadows and Z mountains swarm with our

Coefficients, titillating the sights and sounds, but

Never truly changing the world around us.

What pleasures exist in this world?

That of Eigen satisfaction!

We eat kernels and attend the finest styling of
matrices.

An institute of groupings and cinematography.

For our children, toys of splendor fill their day.

A vast array of light

Produces a spectrum onto their minds,

With a candid frequency.

What can be said of us is this:

Our boundaries lie within the limits

Of our rhythmic souls.

We quantum leap gracefully diffracting quotients

Into multiples of infinity.

To an extent we possess validity,

Ultimately we are the zero point.

Hey Lemon,

I don't think people recognize the things that usually go on outside their microscopic worlds. A whole lot would get done if someone pushed themselves to simply ask, 'What's out there?' It's really a problem.

It's a problem to read about the terrible things that go on in the big world and to see them acted out when I go outside to my small world. It tells me not a whole lot has changed in humanity, and habits are hard to break in a simple work week.

Since my younger years, feelings guided me toward certain events. They provided a way to move without overanalyzing but, along the way, the jabs and stabs from onlookers led me to think about my actions and its warranted effects. Because of that I never really leave my little, imaginary grassy island of the mind, miles away from the city where the skies form into darkness without a moment's hesitation. I like staying on that island, where the hut is nice and warm, the tree gives good shade, the grass is not too prickly, and my tea stays warm in the noontime sun. But the city can never be avoided. I need to go there to see what's happening, to fetch supplies, and to take in local delights. Moreover, I like to see why my grass is greener.

The city is a tough place, to say the least. There's a lot going on and yet nothing happens. Buzzwords float around and obstruct rationale. On occasion, they lead me places I usually don't tend to go. 'For the sake of adventure!' that's what I tell myself, with guile and glee, to push down the nagging, logical thoughts that all mankind keep within to stay alive. The moment I snapped out of it I realized what the matter is and how I strayed from it, all because of the little things that society believed important. It was a distraction.

Usually, I keep my head low and stay to streets that are familiar with a slight detour every once in a while. But I choose not to stay too long since the city can make me restless and edgy. Though I don't mind staying inside the café at the far border of the city, it has good lemonade. Regardless, I exit back onto the grassy island.

It's safe there. No one comes by and the place is quiet. This is my little world and I try to notice what's going on inside. Where the utensils are, whether the fireplace has enough wood, how many steps are from the kitchen to the bathroom, where the mouse holes used to be, so on and so on...? It's easy to miss things though, but I still try. I want to know if everyone else still tries too.

Those people in the city... Do they know how prickly my grass is? I hope not. That would mean they came here or that they're thinking about everything beyond the city, which would lead them to me. I don't want them here. I can do the things I want to do here without the need for extra courage or drugs, for that matter.

You see, when alone I have the passion. A drive that helps me get up from my bed, walks me to the bathroom, helps me slice lumber, and propels me forward on the stretches of land I have. But in the city, it's immediately squashed by the personas that float around with their own desires and histories in tow. I find it overwhelming. Each step dwarfs my motivation since so many people feel pride and courage for whatever their activities are, regardless of its stance as right or wrong. It's a bit confusing. And makes me question whether or not I have done this to myself. I wonder how many people in the city question themselves.

But there is something to be said about those who can wander inside the wild crowds and not be affected. It's impressive. But right now, that's not me. It's good to have little bit of quiet to organize your thoughts.

Whenever I get out of the city I try to take a moment to look upwards and see how the sky is. Inside the city, the buildings and advertisements don't let in too much sunlight. The only reason I knew it was still light out was the motorized purring of the 8:15 bus to Central-West. But outside, I don't even need to look up. The clear environment can already tell me what is going on and the breeze keeps me occupied as I make my trek back to the hut.

...I guess that's all I have to say.

Nothing else is streaming through this mind anymore. I'm going to bed.

(The Lemon wiggles on the plate.)

Some Time

You could say my separation from the city was brought upon through sheer coincidences. But then I'd just have to tell you that you're wrong. Simply put, it was the amalgamation of events that I brought into existence through sheer ignorance. It was guided by the exuberance of enthusiasm. In order:

During my tenure in the city, I hurried to the bus stop. Waiting, I let the world pass by becoming invisible to everyone but the one I wanted to be with. The moon rose, the sun set, and the clouds paced themselves throughout the day. Now it is Yesterday and I see you stroll on by with a smile and a fancy step. You say goodbye without a second glance. There is nothing there but the stream of city folk.

Where was that energy that guided me here? Did it discharge into the ground, finding its way towards the core or was it a fabricated thought that gently hypnotized me? That feeling is creeping up on me. The city folk offer up their condolences with apathetic stares as the bus rolls by dropping off the other citizens. The last question that escapes my

mind right now is, 'what to do Today'? It's
essentially everywhere. I can't escape it so
something must be done about it, the wistful gift
that is the Present.

I guess, I can walk.

The Fall of the Wei

Crossing Heaven's River

With the Crimson Cliffs behind

Peace is not far away.

In the constellation of Unity

Are the stars of Pi and Zhi

The remaining pillars of Wei.

In this last siege, I sing a song

Of the boundless ocean

Of the sun blessing day

Northern Winds! Carry me

To the Gates of Jade

Where I will sit and rest

With joy in my heart

Cao Cao 魏王
King of Wei

Ambush on the Shu Encampment

The summer leaves shade our travels in the forest.

My men wane under the sun's heat.

As night veils the sky

The moon watches over.

The fire intrudes upon us.

My men stand their ground against the flames

Of the uninvited revolution.

Using the Art of Insanity,

My adversaries come with malice and fervor

The people of this land need their savior,

To deliver them from the corruption of the enemy.

If I must die now let the people know

That a hero of the three kingdoms

Will protect them

As he awaits his troops at the Jade Gates.

Liu Bei 劉備
Emperor of Shu Han

The Long, Horrific Triumph of Wu

Quan, smile please. This kingdom will rise under the Sun.

The words of my brother

Pass silently through my heart

The throne I sit on

He built with sharp blade and mind

Now I must nurture this land

With honor and nobility

Sun Quan 孫權
Great Emperor of Wu

The people, the places, Trowa and the monkey[†]

The young man minding his time,

The wrinkly woman poised and lively,

The bald man adjusting his cap,

The young woman with white haired & two-dollar bag,

Trowa and the monkey take the train with these people.

The homeless begging for change,

The filthy bearded man selling 5¢ newspapers,

The old man shouting the past at passersby,

[†] The last 3 pieces (Wei, Shu, and Wu) and this one reflect my Owner's overall experiences after the festival. I found them disheartening as peace wasn't permanent but brief. The 3 earlier pieces speak on China's romantic history ruminating on the defeat and triumphs that pervaded the land. The emperors of each land had their reasons for ruling and conquering. My owner tried to reconcile his history with these events by imagining the end of lives. This piece however describes the journey abroad with a slant. The monkey is his troubles manifested. The people represent, simply, the world. The character didn't prosper. The monkey, his problems, stayed around as my Owner kept dwelling on the war. He wouldn't continue with specifics. He kept mentioning the people and how he almost related to them after the fact. It wasn't hopeful.

The tattooed druggies in the pit piercing
their pain away,

Trowa and the monkey watch these people in the
Square.

The prep-school boys with coiffed hair,

The saucy girls with dynamic skirts,

The worn out teachers with stained mugs,

The unseen advisors,

Trowa and the monkey attend University with these
people.

Those who maimed and broke hearts,

Those who kissed and never told,

Those who walked with eyes down,

Those with darkened skies as backdrops,

Trowa and the monkey listen to their sorrowful
songs.

The astonished girlfriend in the clouds,

The bewildered boyfriend in the tree,

The monotonous drone that cracked a smile,

The paranoid android who finally relaxed,

The green dancer who found life worthless,

These people found Trowa in the cave weeping with his consoling monkey.

The bard with nothing to say,

The horseman with nowhere to go,

The ninja with the clumsy fingers,

The best man with no groom,

The bridesmaid with no bride,

Trowa and the monkey joined them in support group.

The pool holding a tidal wave,

The room with never-ending heat,

The hill with yellow snow,

The sky with two moons,

The planet supporting the giant elm,

Trowa and the monkey collapse in wonderment at these places.

The women with hips and tattoos,

The women in boots and stockings,

The women with kids and wives,

The women with jobs and grit,

The women with books and swords,

Trowa and his monkey look up to these women.

The men with capes and hats,

The men with husbands and cats,

The men who cry in the dark,

The men who wish to see God,

The men who share all,

Trowa and the monkey sit with these men at the table.

Trowa and the monkey travel the world. The human wanting, the animal already knowing.

They look each other square in the eyes at each leg of the journey. The monkey asks Trowa, already knowing, 'where's the end?'

Motionless, Trowa doesn't decide.

84

Trowa continues wandering in and out of places and peoples' lives.

The monkey follows. He only departs when Trowa stops traveling.

Essential Evanescence

A cloud of mist blanketed the field around him. Sparkles emanated rich violet, slowly descending towards the earth. There were neither landmarks to recall the place's name nor figures to call upon for help.

The boy was alone, lying on the dirt field. He breathed in the rich haze of the mist. With arms and legs outstretched, as if pinned by shackles, he accepted this spot of ground as his new home.

The hoarse breathing of the boy cut through the silence. The mist continued twinkling overhead.

A familiar voice softly serenaded the area. The mist twinkled then swirled. Like a mighty hand, it lifted the boy. Bit by bit his body joined the mist. With one breath, he...

This piece is unfinished. My Owner decided to leave it alone for one reason: He had no feelings. With no emotions pouring through his fingers to the page, he couldn't effectively complete the piece. That was his major weakness when writing. In order to put weight in his words, he needed to feel the event, to have it upset him. But there was nothing. That is why the boy was still and, I can assume, became nothing. I guess the piece is here to fill space or remind him that he has unfinished work.

Treat Your Life like Gin and Brandy

One glass at time, you drink to your heart's content the misery and sickness of the world. At home, you are a drunk, tending to your thoughtful garden filled with loneliness. In company, you are a gentle friend, making everyone happy by recreating embarrassing sins. The Gin face you make is the overwhelming rush of a new experience, the Brandy jig is the dance of oblivious mortification. As you walk the streets you come across a fellow you call 'friend'. You place your arm around him in such a loving manner only to receive a shove and a finger in reply. You sit in a gutter with sober people's shadows grazing over you with a familiar darkness and wonder what of beer. How would your life have been if beer were the answer? Would you be less sober and live in the moment or possibly not have so many booze grimaces?

Someone then comes up to you asking inane questions adding to your lame questions resulting in a massive headache of curiosity. You wave off the new acquaintance by shouting 'get away from me' and the person asks himself what your deal was. Your deal was you had no friends who cared about you outside the bar. Moreover, you do not go to bars

that much and you tell no one about your problems.
But you need a family so you wander the city looking
for a bar to call home. There is no luck. So you
return to your somber palace in need of Gin to place
your problems in retrospect.

During your cabinet raid, you spy a bottle of wine
from 1920. This makes you wonder what if you were
a wine aficionado and lived through it. Would you
then be sophisticated? Would women want you
more? Would friends come over for something other
than an intervention? You take a gander at your Gin
and Brandy collection strewn across your cubic
rattrap apartment and grow evermore displeased
with your current tastes.

You take the wine bottle as a pillow and peek into
an alternate reality that is Wine.

Look at the lavish books, an impenetrable fortress
that only your brilliant mind can tap into. Posters of
the African Renaissance litter the hallway giving
the impression that you possess intelligence beyond
your socioeconomic bubble. The hallway ends
reaching your kitchen, spotless, and grand. The food
you keep make bones stronger, teeth whiter, breath
fresher, and body happy. You take your fill then step

into your ballroom bathroom to dispose of your waste. Unlike your Gin and Brandy infested bathroom. In the real world there's a mildew-riddled shower/tub, a cockroach entryway that's your sink and a wastebasket doubling as a toilet on those days that you're filled with so much Brandy your eyes create illusions. No, this bathroom makes you feel refreshed after you leave it. Once done, you head towards your spectacular bedroom with a working television, featuring every expensive channel. There's also a brilliant self-portrait of you sans the satire, a bed with pillows decoratively draped by the sweet embrace of your college sweetheart. You glide towards her across your Persian rug on your Fireside slippers. You envelope her with your own warm embrace. That was Monday.

But not here. In the real world, the only woman who calls is the woman who filed the lawsuit against you for that one night of drinking in the streets. The only way to receive nourishment is by swallowing your almost vomited food, leaving the bathroom feeling filthier than ever.

Marriage Material

'I don't know where to go,' he said with a tear scurrying down his cheek, crashing to the hand of the woman holding his face with whatever tenderness was left in her.

'Calm down,' she said, sternly. 'I don't like you, but I can never see you hurt.'

'That makes no sense.'

He pushed away her hand; the tear continued its ride toward his chin. He turned and walked to the door of the small room that housed their pitiful dreams and fidelity. Before placing his hand on the knob, he looked up.

'This is stupid. You're an idiot. If I ever hear you say that to me again, how you hate me yet want me to be safe, he took a breath. I swear to God. I'm tired of this shit.'

'You think I'm not tired too. I'm here. I'm scared just like you are. Just come here.' She opened her arms expecting him to turn back and take shelter inside her warmth like before; just like their honeymoon, just like on their 10th anniversary, and exactly when they lost their baby girl.

Instinctively, he turned and noticed the half-hearted smile on her face.

'Don't,' he exclaimed. Blood flooding his fists as he punched the wall. 'Don't you dare!' He walked back to the door. 'I don't want to repeat this again and again. You hurt me, in your little ways, I punch another wall. I hurt you, you demean and it never works. Nothing works! We sniped at each other on our honeymoon, we can't rely on each other, and we haven't touched since she died.' Finally, turning the knob, he left.

Holding her cheek, all the truths sunk in. All the belittling bouts, washed away and the anger rose to the surface. Adrenaline coursed through her veins but her body remained stationary. The sudden shock of him leaving made her feel like that downtrodden little girl again, plotting desperately for her father's attention. A small tear rolled down her cheek as she was left to attend to the feelings for her newly deceased father.

The Crumbling Office [*]

"That account's been our bread and butter since the early 90's and we were only able to meet those three Executives because of that account. Now you're telling me we lose the account to some small shit firm with a bunch of fags running around sucking each other off?"

The Assistant opened his mouth to answer.

"No, I don't want to hear it. Keep your mouth shut, stay here, and listen." The Manager reached over to grab the receiver of his office phone but not before shoving aside a couple of anonymous folders, papers, and other important looking material. Each hit of the phone keypad punctuated the Assistant's heartbeat. "Hello? May I speak to Cunningham, he knows who I am."

A few moments later, a chipper tone spewed pleasantries into the Manager's ear.

The Manager's demeanor changed from vitriolic to amiable. "I don't need to hear it Cunningham, every time you start to talk about

---

[*] This short story is true. Everything said and felt was in real time. He fought hard to be this normal. One decade of organization, people-pleasing, & hollow lunches, he purposefully got laid off by egging his boss's wife. No jail time as the boss joined for a throw. With free time, he built & moved into the cabin that we now reside in. His daughter didn't approve but she understood like many children aware that their parents had lives before their time do.

Bills and their game play, I tell you about the Eagles and their defensive lineman. We both know this is gonna last for about an hour so let's just say right now that we're both right. Can we do that? ... Anyway, I called because of something I heard through the grapevine over here...Yeah, why is that? We're not doing good enough work for you," his tone shifted into biting sarcasm. "...We have been with you for years and now you're going to another firm...You still haven't told me why you're moving your business away from us," he pointed to a chair, forcing the Assistant to sit. "So you're telling me that finances are paramount compared to quality and loyalty? ...No, you can't just get out of a deal whenever you feel like it...That's too bad. Listen, I have the right to seek certain action on this—No, NO, STOP, WE HAD A DEAL AND IT WILL DESTROY YOUR COMPANY IF YOU GET AWAY FROM IT. DON'T BACK OUT NOW...Fine, see what happens in the next five years without us to save your asses!"

"What are you looking at," his temper shifted toward the Assistant.

With as much meekness as a newborn cat, he said, "You told me to stay."

"Whatever. Well, now you know what happens in business. People shit all over you until they can't shit no more or they can't stand the smell. Then they leave. And that's what happened right now. That account just walked up, sat on our faces, did its business, then moved along to the next target."

"Maybe we can still get them back. Do you know why they would leave?"

"MONEY. They apparently offer a better service for a cheaper price. It's only going to get them in trouble since that Company only did to snatch them up and get more from them later on. It's the old Free Sample Gambit. Write that down, you'll need it someday."

The Assistant scratched ink on a free page.

The Manager wiped his face. "Alright, get back to work or whatever it is you do. Me and the boys are gonna mull over this."

Leaving his superior's presence, Assistant went off to the corridor of cubicles. His desk had the supposed essentials cluttering the beige landscape. Several water bottles taking up space in the corner, some tissues to wipe his nose, three-hole punch, a stapler, notebook paper with some pieces containing curvy text, and a desktop computer, resonating a winter glow from the first day he turned it on 10 years ago.

A Story between Wolf and Cub

It was yester night that we had our talk on the grass
outside our cabin. We looked up at the night sky as
the tiny green pins were crushed under our weight. I
pointed to The Big and Little Dippers, Orion's Belt,
and The Three Wise men and told her where their
names came from.

She wrinkled her round nose at the thought. Her
long braids provided an obstacle for traveling ant
and, though it was faint, I could see her dark, brown
eyes counting and tracking each dot in the sky. She
did look a lot like her, especially the mocha skin.
That's what made it easier to tell her that she was
beautiful. Nevertheless, I would hold myself back
and tell her she looks just like her mother. It seemed
to make her happy enough.

I went on explaining the cosmos, how Earth's
knowledge only extends to the borders of our galaxy
and how everything else is just calculated
speculation.

Her lungs ballooned in her chest then deflated
quickly. Obviously, she was getting bored.

"What's the matter," I asked.

"I don't wanna know about all that."

"What do you mean 'you don't wanna know about all
that?' That is important for you to know," I said,
waving my hands at the heavens. She's always been
interested in the fantastic, why be disinterested
now?

"Right now, it's boring. I wanna talk about
something else. The stars will always be there."

"Alright, what else is there?" A full moment passed
by before a good idea came to me. "Tomorrow, the
weatherman said it was going to rain." I grinned.

"That's even worse than stupid space," she
bellowed. "Tell me something interesting like when
you and mom met."

I simply looked at her. She asked me this exact
question before and I immediately tell her what I
told her before. 'We met at the library, we talked,
then some years later we got married and had you.
There. Happy now?' She didn't buy it then and it
didn't seem like she bought it now.

My daughter, a stubborn little child in a sundress, asked again where her mother and I met and wanted to know what I first thought of her. "Well, tell me."

"I thought she was nice."

"That's it," she asked, unconvinced.

"Yeah and at that same library we read up on how Black Holes carry the possibility of transporting you across space and, possibly, time? And that the nearest one to Earth is--"

"If I get inside one now will it take me to a time and place where you answer my question?" She snapped. Her wide-eyed expression implored me.

I rolled my eyes. "If you're going to get so sassy, I don't think I'll tell you."

"Plenty of other kids in homeroom know how their parents met. Jamie's parents met at a funfair and fell in love at the elephant ride. Malcolm's moms went to the same high school and moved away to college. They got an apartment together. Five years later, they were married. All I get to say is my parents met at a library. What else happened?"

"We fell in love then had you. End." I closed my eyes.

"Stop it! Now it's annoying. Why won't you tell me?"

"You're not old enough yet to hear it, not the real version anyway," I said with a matter-of-fact attitude.

She crossed her arms and let out a pout. We both laid there for a few minutes before I caved in.

"Up north, near your grandparents' house, you know the churchyard you love so much, the one with the lilies planted there every spring? Around 12 years ago, there was a bus stop across that street and that's where I would see your mom every now and then. I worked in the building a few blocks down and whenever I ended my shift I would see her there, waiting for the stop like everyone else."

"So you lied? There's was no library?" She snapped.

"Nah, told you that to make me sound smart."

"Oh." She wrinkled her nose. "And then you said 'hi' to her?"

"No, I merely noticed." I sat up, shaking the grass clippings from my hair. "It wasn't until it rained that she noticed me. The bus was early that day and I don't run for buses at all. But it stopped halfway towards the light at the corner and I jogged to get it. She was at the front of the bus, with a smile telling me, 'that was a close one.' I walked over and sat across telling her thanks for stopping the bus, blah, blah. It was the few ways I could've talked to her."

"What were the other ways?"

"I don't know. It already happened, there's no use in worrying about it."

She scooched over and rested on my arm. "So, what next? You asked her out?"

"No, I just talked to her for a little while. Well, actually she talked to me. It seemed like she noticed me before, I guess that's why she was so comfortable. It seems dumb when I think about it, how a facial tick would inspire me to walk over a whole bus length. There was really no guarantee that she liked me in any way. It was just a chance I took."

"Malcolm's mom said that she took the same kind of chance. That's when she found out how much his other mom liked her. There didn't seem like any other way for you to do it," she said, looking up at me with those little brown eyes.

"That's true. We saw each other the next day and she didn't get back to her home that night." I coughed after realizing my allusion. Her face suggested only acknowledgment of her mother not going home so I continued. "The next day, we sat outside during my lunch break and talked about the most inane things but we enjoyed it. At the end, I finally asked her out on a real date. I left with the biggest smile on my face."

"That sounds sappy, pappy," she said as she grabbed both my biceps with her spindly fingers. "But I don't understand why you wouldn't tell me this before?"

"There's more. Since that day, we were never really apart, except for the little vacations she had with her family, or the road trips I took with your aunt down the coast. I never got tired of seeing her. But, we eventually hit our saturation point. About a year and three months in, it was about summer at this point, we were living together for almost five months. And we were just staring each other down at the table. Remember the photos of the apartment I showed you?"

She nodded.

"It was there, right there, that we had our worst argument. I couldn't for the life of me understand what she was angry about but that didn't surprise me. Your mother had a way of speaking in cryptic messages for no reason at all. I kept telling her that I didn't understand. I wanted to fix it if only she would tell me what the problem was, but that just made things worse and she left. She moved back in with her parents two days later."

"What did you do?"

"I called and called but she ever picked up. I tried getting in touch with here over the next week. Every time I went to her parent's home, she was 'never home'. I didn't know what to do after that."

She moved in sitting between my legs, leaning back with her head resting on my chest. "I'm sorry."

"What are you sorry about? It wasn't your fault."

"Duh, I just know how you feel."

"Oh, really?" I said with my chin slightly digging into her head.

"Well, there was a boy named Jamie in my class that I liked, but he moved away and I never got his address. So, I know what it feels like to like someone but they're never there."

I blinked twice. "You can't have a boyfriend until you're eighteen. Got it?"

She sighed. "Got it. Now tell me the rest of the story."

"Well, I took a new job across town and left it all behind me. I rearranged the apartment, I reacquainted myself with old friends and recent ones, and I lived. Two months past and your aunt, how can I put this, forced me to come to her friend's birthday party."

103

"She wanted to get drunk so she wouldn't have to drive herself home."

"Yes and do not mention anything about that to her when you see her next week. Moving on, you know what happens at birthday parties. There were greetings, cake, presents, the forced feeling of celebration for another year, the same old stuff. Throughout, I mingled with my sis' friends and found only one to talk with. Her name was Hazel and we spent the better part of the evening chatting until she left. I then brought your mom home, like I usually did, and after coming back from walking her up I saw Hazel across the street. We waved to each other and met in the middle of the street and before I knew it we were kissing."

Her eyes widened. "YOU KISSED SOMEONE ELSE?"

"I was surprised then as you are now. When we stopped, she said she's been wanting to do that since we met. I told her that I wasn't ready for anything too real and she agreed. The next week we hung out and it continued--"

"The 'Kissing'?"

"The kissing, yes, the kissing continued." I stopped for a moment to look at her. "Do you want me to continue?"

"Against my better judgment, yes."

"We stopped seeing each other a week later. The same day your mom came back."

"WHAT!? She decides to come back NOW?" Her face scrunched up on the last word causing her to bare her teeth until the last syllable, the 'ow'.

"I couldn't believe it. She was back with luggage in hand. Her puffy face told me everything she went through. The confusion, the anger, the regret. I could only mutter, 'why' before she dropped her bag and hugged me so tight I couldn't get away. I didn't want to." I breathed in the cold night air. My eyes darted between the stars and the ground. It was getting closer to her bedtime, she knew it too, but she wanted me to keep going.

"It was there that I finally understood. Why she left and to where?"

She sat waiting for the punch line. "Why'd she leave?"

"She couldn't conceive. She said, 'I could never be a mother and I wanted to be with you but I thought you would not accept me like this.' Tears were streaming down her face as she told me from across the table. I held out my hand. I told her to put hers in mine. I said, 'I would never abandon you. I would support you with everything that I am, with all my faults and strengths. Don't think for a damn second that that isn't true.' She squeezed my hand tighter and I pulled her in for a kiss. We stayed together from then on. And with the help of a friend of mine, we were able to have you."

She sniffed and hid her head on my chest. She never wanted people to see her cry. "I can't believe you told me that." She muffled. "I just wanted to know how you met, not everything!" She pushed me away and ran back into the cabin.

I didn't want to hurt her. That is why I always said we met at a library. It's short and sweet and ends, predictably, but happily.

SECTION III: THE OLD MAN AND HIS CAT

1/1/05

I sit in the car finding resolution from the chaos by gazing at those dancing, blinding lights outside. I picture myself among those lights, among the crowd this particular evening. Content patrons wedge past with their top hats, jester glasses, and sloppy strides. No hostility, no fear, confusion nor sadness among them. Just happiness. For a brief moment a smile creeps upon my face. It's confusing and odd since I don't celebrate. There is nothing fantastic about tonight. The radio is on with the odd telling of an odd universe filled with odd adventures of regularly baffled people. I listen and smoke as the story unfolds about a character, a precarious boy, who is his own god. My face and body relax as the smoke escapes my throat through the open window. In the past, suspense filled the evening in the destitute part of my home as the radio droned on as I sat in my listening chair. But not now. The car begins its travel away from the crowds, into the night. Something within me changed. I shrug it off, but the feeling steadies. The car rides along bringing my soul into some void. The jauntiness behind me lessens and the night darkens. In the beginning the gaiety was apparent, the crowd drunk-walks with

110

happy faces, arms draped over shoulders, and cries
of past mistakes finally forgotten. Now I sense the
pain of drunkenness. Bright red cheeks in pain the
moment the clock resets. Our speed provides a
decent barrier to such pain. But the moment the
engine stops and the door unlocks and I step onto
my sidewalk, those feelings will stun me without
fail. Following is an immediate shutdown of my
systems, then regret. For now, I am safe. This night
is the most celebrated. This pain persists and we
continue to face it no matter how it personifies. Now
the lights are off and the evil stops growing. The car
slows at a yield. I rest, hoping for energy. 'Why is it
that I have not died yet?' My car then quickens as I
struggle with the question. I leave it for another day
and ride along to not be late for my program. It
distracts from the holiday pain. I guess that's why I
am alive. The odd stories of the odd universe show
me the world in its entirety. I cannot miss it, not
this year. We reach our destination. The barrier
lowers. The agony seeps in. I step onto the sidewalk,
feeling the pain creep up my leg but... cannot stop
until I listen to my programs. Barely make it to the
front door, to home, safe from chaos. The jacket goes

on the rack, the pipe sits between my lips, and the radio blinks on. I plop onto my chair.

Right on time.

1/7/05

My cat accompanied me on my trip to the
supermarket, I couldn't do it alone. We first got the
carriages and walked straight towards the batteries.
It's the only thing my cat wanted for today. Mine
was an extensive list: Cereal (Rice Krispies), meat,
vegetables, and milk. He was now at the counter
buying AA batteries, with his little purse in mouth,
full of quarters, checking the new issue of
'Seventeen' magazine to be informed on what's hot
and what's not. I, occasionally, despise that literary
bullshit. I moved ahead, passing the lettuce patch,
veering into the frozen food aisle. The low
temperature of frozen peas and carrots was no
bother. Their icy box art invited gourmet chefs for a
little kitchen 'fun in the sun'. That reminds me, I
need waffles. Where did this Aunt Jemima come
from, and where has she been all my life? Does she
embody the black woman cook of breakfast treats? If
so there are too many ragamuffins making dinner.
People shouldn't be so shy and squeamish with
interracial cooking; it's fun to have lasagna with
tacos. My cat is now trying to haggle with the clerk,
bringing the price of batteries down to $1.98. He's a
nice negotiator. I ran out of ketchup weeks ago.

Mayonnaise's little brother is so popular with spaghetti. Mustard is just too bossy on my hot dog. My cat brings it down to $1.25. As I walk to the cereal aisle for my Rice Krispies, a young woman with her Old Navy full of sorrow smiled at me. Her demeanor was that of a mother too tired to smile but did it anyway. I smiled with pearly whites through my long beard. This young, thin woman, as if walking on broken glass, approached me. We dashed to the dairy aisle and fornicated. My cat got it down to $.68. Her supple bosom large and full of fresh milk smothered my beard. My cat got it down to $.59. I reached around for her pale crescent moon. Quite small, it was. When squeezed it molds between my fingers. She wrapped herself around me, making her legs a belt, arms and hands up and down my back. My cat is now down to $.32. I was in her for what seemed like two minutes then stopped. I was first. I am too old for jaunty stamina, more for listless stamina. We recaptured our composure, said our farewells, and she slipped on her Old Navy now with satisfaction along with her number and bra. I pushed my cart to the counter and discovered my cat bought the batteries for $.12. I am very proud. As I spent $300.19 on my things, the lady spent $69.92

on hers. In my cart, a can of squash, peas, and carrots, waffles, mustard (I said screw you to ketchup), Razzle Dazzle Rice Krispies, and 2% milk and a bra. She bought a piece of my soul, pancakes, broccoli and eggplants, ketchup (she can't stand the royal attitude of mustard), and Cinnamon Toast Crunch. My cat spent 1% of his allowance this week. I am very proud of him. I was surprised at the woman/mother, giving away her milk in the dairy aisle. I hope during next year's visit there won't be so much bargaining.

1/15/05

My cat had quite an adventure today, or was it yesterday? Either way, he had quite a day. Or so he told me. As he tells it, the day began when he awoke. About 4 a.m. it was, as he told me. Peeling away the gritty glue connecting his eyelids, he had a sudden craving for fish. To satisfy this craving he took his old fishing pole and rode to the lake. He is a very experienced bike rider, learning at the age of two. During the ride, he felt a hot hiss on his neck. It was harsh with the desire to strike him down. He had to do something, knowing that the creature could hurt him if he became too suspicious. So he swerved, slamming the beast into a tree. Looking back, he discovered it was a koala bear. He was so stricken with guilt that he decided to stay with it and nurse it back to health. I'm very proud of him. Moments later, the koala regained himself and lunged at him. Scratching, biting, and tearing at my cat's flesh. It went completely mad. Maybe it wanted a faster ride? My cat usually rides slowly, for the sights. Maybe it didn't have its fix? It is a well-known fact that koala bears go insane without their dose of eucalyptus. During the mauling, he reached for the fishing rod and bashed the bothersome bear

116

over the head. The koala stopped, its paws fruitlessly nursing his wound. With the koala dazed, my cat dashed for the bike and rammed into the bear. The front wheel bent upon impact but it was worth it, according to him. My cat continued toward the lake, with bent wheel and his will exasperated. He was still hungry for some fish too. A quarter of a mile near the lake he crashed into a tree or bush or something, he wasn't really clear. He roughed it the rest of the way with pole in mouth. After reaching the lake, to his surprise, it was dry. Just a huge muddy bowl of a field was left and all the fish gone. He said they went back to their home and got tired of being caught and eaten, he read a note made by them saying, 'So long and thanks for all the worms.' I was a bit skeptical about the note part. Though saddened by their imminent departure he did not let it defer him from finding food. But since it was almost sunrise, he let the sun deter him instead. He headed home, passing his broken bike, passing the broken koala. His hopes of finding a delectable fish were dashed. But a surprise was waiting for him. This is where I come in. A big heaping of flounder, his favorite, was waiting for him on the breakfast table. He dropped his rod and ate heartily. The koala never recovered.

So I was told.

1/19/05 (originally decades before)

After a year of individuality, after bearing the harsh realities of my own temperament, after training to the tune of discipline and prestige, I venture out of the hyperbolic time chamber and into the world. One moment sticks out of my mind as I realize singularity and distinction for the first time in a long time: Dashing the separate personality from my self. How did the personality come to be? Simple, it was a process of great turmoil and imagination. My stay in the chamber was not life threatening or gruesome. The other personality passes the time faster, in fact made the affair more pleasant. During the days, I train to the point of exhaustion. At night, I rest on the soft, velvety bed, king sized mind you, the better for the other to gain control and comfortably perform his daily activities. Furthermore, when I am not training or he is not doing what he does, the body switched to standby and we conversed through telepathy. The moment I stepped out of that chamber, the whole being went to ruins. What to do with the extra persona? I couldn't leave it nor could I continue with the above procedure. Not outside. The only solution was destruction. Then the question becomes, how could I go through destroying something that became someone? This discolored thread in the fabric of my own persona. I will take the risk, but still hesitate. What if he replaced me? I have that particular fear of being substituted by my better and cast aside like an old fridge. I can barely handle the jealousy I have for the next door neighbor. Perhaps it could still be done. Besides, how would the battle pan out? Maybe a mental warfare is too bizarre for my taste. But the question still stands. Clearly I do not have the know-how or the audacity to destroy a mental figure with complexities and mannerisms similar or contrary to my own. Besides, I might need someone to quarrel with at home.

2/14/05

I decided to go outside today. My cat, with his bag full of cards, accompanied me. The world is under pressure right now to convey feelings not yet thoroughly understood. I placed myself at the center off all of this, between the haves and have not's, deciding to witness the extravagant bazaar of bags full of petals, arms clutching plush animals, eyes endlessly wanting, and of course the cute idioms on cards. I expected splashes of red but I saw the usual colors strewing about and adorned. Not even a distinguishable air about people, just normality. They must be hiding it. As I rested on a store porch step, as my cat exchanged gifts of pleasure to strangers on the street, I noticed a very melancholy girl. Nothing too peculiar about her. It was just that she was crying over a gift she received. My cat ran over and entrusted her with his last card. I was very proud of him. She was puzzled, bewildered, happy, and then satisfied. She got up, with a new kick in her step and sped off to somewhere or maybe someone. Feeling a cramp creep up my leg, I ventured further into the city. No one was around, did I miss something? I spotted a couple in their one-floor house committing intercourse. So I did miss something. I guess a memo from the government telling everyone to fornicate or face a month in prison, at least that's what I and my cat concluded. So as not to be an odd man out, I decided to find someone, but first finding a gift. It is more appropriate to give a gift then ask as oppose to just asking with nothing in hand. My cat and I wrote dozens of idioms on cards and decided on one. It contained the phrase: *I'd hitchhike the galaxy for to gaze into your eyes*. It had a drawing of a stick figure hitchhiking on a planet. I thought it was superb, my cat thought it could've been better. Now to find a woman to have sex with. During our walk, I saw potential. Some were too tall or short, others were too skinny or fat, and many already had someone. After a while, I eventually found someone. She had jet black hair, a nice frame, actual meat on her bones, breasts big but not too big, and she had no one. There was some skepticism made by my cat, he thought she might not like a man with a wizard's beard. I shooed away his comment and proceeded to give her the gift. She saw me walking towards her, cringed for a bit then took a liking to me. I presented her the hitchhiker's card and she absolutely adored it. We went back to her house, which was a block

away, and had sex. After about four hours, we
proceeded to talk about things. My cat waited on the
stoop. She told me she hated today. The reason she
slept with me was because I was a good guy not just
because of today. I said thank you. She continued by
saying that she was waiting for someone else but he
took too long. So she settled for the nice guy with the
card. Handmade card, I emphasized. Then she told
me that the guy was probably there but she didn't
care. I put my clothes on and left thanking her for
the evening. She obliged. As I walked back I spotted
a man with a pocket watch. No gift, just time and
nervous patience.

3/01/05

It is winter time now. The season's only for a
weekend. Since I decided to live by myself, with my
cat, I devoted the winters to finding a temporary job.
My cat dislikes this ritual, believing my hips will
turn into edges of a desk, my face and eyes morph
into a projector presenting a steady clock ticking
back and forth showing no end to the day. I
discarded his comment, ate my buttered toast and
went for a job search. There was a need for a job
during this cold season. It brings vitality to my old
bones; with a job there's purpose of being and
purpose to open your eyes to the world around you.
Besides if I don't I'll be staring at my fireplace all
weekend. I proceeded to the Job Placement Bureau
by foot and waited in the dizzying line for the Grand
Master of Defining an Individual's Purpose. He is
also known as a job placement counselor. Personally,
they were clueless buffoons, deciding your fate by
which kind of animal you'd most likely have dinner
with. An imbecile, with no room for intelligence, has
plenty of space for 'deep' thought. As I walked to the
office nothing seemed surreal. It was odd, to say the
most. Cautiously, I gazed the room, hoping for a
surprise here and there, but no. It was a plain room,

with a plain man, in a plain short-sleeved shirt, tie, and khakis. I felt sorry for him. The moment I sat down he bellowed a great sigh for his humanity and job placement. After the Assessment Hour, my winter job was found: The prime minister of Malaysia. It was nothing to cheer about, but it did give me some insight on my personality and the test. Instead of going out of the office and pursuing my winter job, I stayed and assessed the job placement counselor. After a rigorous 70 hours of spirit evaluation and questions pertaining to which different colored ink Kim Jong Un would like to write with, a dream job was discovered. His excitement was palpable. He found his calling, his raison d'être, that subject he can bore people at parties with. He would set out to become a Cacti Florist. As much as I tried to calm him down, he couldn't stop jumping towards the ceiling. I believe understating fantastic events help maintain composure for your person. After helping him sign termination papers and changing his worldview, we left the Bureau and pursued our respective winter jobs. I was proud of myself. After the weekend came Spring. I passed in my two weeks' notice for Prime Minister. The job was cushy with only one instance of an assassination attempt. I walked home hoping my cat didn't scratch my good wooden chair or throw any parties. Along the way, I spotted two giant robots battling, and the black one was winning. The white one never stood a chance. I guess those people found good jobs for themselves. I opened the front door. A broken piñata welcomed me with penny prizes strewn about leading to the day room. I sighed and patted my cat's head.

3/04/05

A penguin friend of my cat came to stay for a while last month. He left ten minutes ago. His story of arrival was grand. He waited several hours at the Fairbanks International airport because of a frozen wheel on one of their planes. Flying in the air, a terrorist group threatened every passenger if they weren't brought to California. They were promptly pushed off. I was surprised to hear this. Usually we tie them up then throw them off the plane. After that ordeal, Harry, his name in penguin was 'lover of all trees', hailed a cab and drove to our house. He wasn't much for adventures, he said, but the flight was delightfully enthusiastic. During his stay, him and my cat got reacquainted and started from where they left off. They were college roommate's junior year, participants in an interspecies experiment to see if two people from different places could get along. I never had any of that when I was young. Yesterday, they went to an amusement park to see what it was all about. When they got there the fireworks already started, it was 1:45pm. They went on the carousal first to get the hang of things. My cat was excited. Harry didn't like it much. He had no opinion of horses but still wished not to ride them.

Afterwards, they tried a rollercoaster. My cat was not a fan of heights but with his fantastic ability to land he risked it. As they waited in line they talked about the past and present. My cat learned Harry's present, about his wife and children, his new job, and how the years treated him. He, supposedly, runs a law firm in Alaska that deals with the prosecution of big Ice Cube Companies and how they don't claim responsibility for the damages made by their cubes in drive-by accidents. It's quite a complex field. His wife and three kids are proud of his work. The wife works as a schoolteacher, she teaches P.E. They make a nice living. When it was their turn for the rollercoaster the blood drained from my cat's body. He fainted onto his companion. It was the Superman© ride at Six Flags now that I remember. He heard gruesome stories of riders decapitated, passengers rocketing off into the confection stands, and vomit racing to the end just to hit your face. When he came to, he verbally wondered what if it happens to him. Harry eased those worries and helped him onto the car. They described the ride in two different ways: My cat said it was treacherous and hazardous, his friend on the other hand said it was so boring only comatose person would enjoy it. I didn't get it. Anyway, after the ride they ate corndogs, chilidogs, hot dogs, sour dogs, funny dogs, and drank some soda. During the walk back home they talked some more about the good old days. They reminisced about this and that and felt joy. It is somewhat remarkable how memories stay, letting us only see what has been instead of visiting it physically. I have those once in a while whenever I bump my head on the bathroom sink. Twenty minutes ago they exchanged hugs and ate some dinner. Upon his leave my cat told me at first he didn't like Harry. As they continued living with each other, he started to see that all penguins weren't just math wizards.

3/05/05

A woman gave me her number earlier today and I haven't called her yet. She is just as old as I am but with lighter hair. I talked to my cat about this and he told me to call at my leisure, in other words an hour from now. She was pretty. I met her at the park bench where I usually mock the ducks for their squalor. She sat next to me and agreed. They looked perfect on the outside, but their nests and finances were atrocious. I proclaimed it was true. They seem like complete obsessive compulsives when you're around. We talked a little bit more about ducks, hamsters, and the increase appearance of giant robots. Surprisingly intelligent she was, so I invited her to the library. We chose our books and discussed which were better. I haven't been delighted like this in a quinquennium. She chose 'Hitchhiker's Guide to the Galaxy' by Douglas Adams. I chose 'The Once and Future King' by T.H. White. We couldn't decide which was better. We said why not both at the same time and let our eyes linger on each other's faces: noting the curve of the jaw, its connection to her reddening cheeks, juxtaposing her pale nose bending the skin around the eyes. Her hazel-jade eyes. We turned away and walked through the same park and

saw the same ducks acting proper. We walked
through the boulevard of shattered wishes and
glanced at the day star. When we made it to her
house, made of wood, like mine, she asked if I
wanted to come in. I replied with a yes. Upon
entering I felt the presence of a dog. A very
discerning one at that. My cat taught me how to
sense one without needing to neither see, smell,
hear, nor touch. And he was definitely a dog. She
said he was a bit overprotective and wary of
strangers. I wasn't surprised. My cat is the same
way. I appreciated the dog's gesture. As we sat and
drank tea, the dog interrogated me with the
demeanor of a hardened, private dick. I answered
them as truthfully as I could. That seemed to please
the dog. She was mortified, however. I told her it
was ok. An hour of questions later, he told me that I
was ok. I can stay and potentially date his master.
Her cheeks beamed volcano red. The dog went back
to his small shack in the yard. My date and I
continued to talk about stuff. I liked that her dog
assumed our future courtship. I was thinking about
it too. Later, she walked me back to the park, with
the now leashed dog following behind. She said she
had a nice time and how she only had so-so times up

until now. It made the day more special. I said goodbye as well, turned, and started to walk when she pulled me back. She put a piece of paper on my palm, creating a cage of fingers around it. Her and her dog quickly strode off in the opposite direction and I, gleeful, walked towards my house. The moment I told my cat about her, he didn't believe me. Dogs ask much more questions than an hour's worth, he said. I shrugged at the comment, paying more attention to her number and when I should call. An hour has almost past and I still don't know. All I know is this; she had orange hair, pale skin, nice eyes, a defensive dog, and a special 'nice' day which were different from the rest.

3/08/05

The women of this land, I noticed, are relatively complex but overall quite simple like a shoelace, with twists and turns that repeat into beautiful designs. I discussed this notion with my cat and he merely shrugged at the idea. He doesn't know much about women, he doesn't get out much. I've learned from experience of their humanity but I couldn't quite describe the difference between them and men. Yesterday, I went out to get some insight on this. I figured talking to women would be great start. As I proceeded to create a discussion I was slapped, scolded, spit on, or looked at with bewilderment. It was quite bothersome. Eventually, I found someone to talk to. He, or it is more appropriate to say she, was a transsexual. She took a break from her work and walked with me to the coffee shop. It was a good setting for a philosophical, gender-related, conversation. Her name was Beretta, a philanthropist. We sat down and began our discussion with a series of questions. She answered by telling me that some women do what they do in order to survive on this planet. She asked me, 'Have you ever experienced a man fully?' I replied, 'Yes and no. I've been with men in war, to drink, during

133

birth, and death, and tax time. But never sexually or for long term romance.' 'Well,' she replied. 'It's very hard, like being with a fussy baby or a try-hard plumber who can barely fix your pipes. It's frustrating how many explored this universe but deny the existence of a women's pleasure center. Or to find that sweet men will disparage women because of loneliness. So, with this behaviour in the forefront of our minds, women survive by protecting themselves, being aggressive, leaning in,' she rolled her eyes at that saying, 'understanding femininity and defining it. Essentially, maturing on a metaphysical level. The only way to survive is to realize your soul. A lot of men don't do this properly. I've found that they look at a lot of material possession, monikers, and activities for sense of self. How do you define your masculinity?' I thought for a moment and defined it as such: The good things that I do, filled with integrity, benefit myself and others while the bad things I do, filled with indecency, are done seldom and learned from. That's the best I can come up with. A lot of women apparently do that already, but not many men. She continued, 'That's disheartening. One thing is I don't think there much of a general difference between the sexes. We experience the same trials and B.S. as the other. The toxic devil is in the details. We face different beauty standards that ultimately limit our physical expression. No man can be elegant without power; no woman can be powerful without sexiness. We face intellectual standards differently. Men are assumed to know about the technical and mathematical; women are assumed to know about health and domestic chores instinctively. Even the privileges we obtain from birth. A boy growing up is immediately set on a course for physical and intellectual exploration but is never prepared for emotional exploration. This is opposite for the girl where emotional and social exploration are paramount. It always rubs me the wrong way whenever I think about my own past.

At this point, time decided that this was enough information for the afternoon. We exchanged farewells and she went back out on the street as I walked back home. Throughout my walk I noticed various interactions that I was out of my view. A man subtly ignoring his girlfriend who pines for him. Another man taking a verbal beating from his girl, wearing a bewildered look I know all too well. A group of men wondering what they were missing, as a group of women discussed what they gain. Maybe both sexes will meet in the middle someday when it comes to their worries.

3/11/05

I had this dream that I was 80 years old again. The age reversal caused me to run for miles in the city. I ran as far as my legs carried me weaving through boulevards and avenues with human shells sitting and drinking coffee. The ventablack liquid plopped straight to their bottoms for lack of organs in the way. My heart pumped all the blood it could before giving out. But I kept running. Discordant ambient light flooded the city streets, the unimportant occupants departed, and the night sky opened up an entryway. This opening summoned a guide in the form of a man in nothing but knee high black sock, underpants, and a decoder ring. We ran through a first floor window; proceed upstairs to some point, noticing baroque workers inside. It was full of aristocratic demons crafting unique qualities on their computers. Nothing gave me the greatest satisfaction than noticing someone's gaudy, melodramatic business and interrupting it. I pass on viewing the 2nd floor show of fire working spectacles concentrating each flare on a latter thought. I notice some man holding his gun to his cheek, speaking of going back to zero on the 33rd floor. We reached the rooftop seeing in the sky a fabulous ghost in a shell

137

absorbing the lights of the far off streets. My pupils dilated to see the event in full. The shell cracked along its sides, hardly enclosing the belittled power. I fainted and... just to remind myself, pick up a bag of salt for the snow outside from the neighbor's house. Continuing on... my body suddenly merged with the building creating a colossal figure controlled by that ghost. Then the dream ends, or my memory of it. There is some manner of analysis my cat told me about to interpret dreams but that only works with dreams consisting of food. So I decided to insert it here but many fragments have crept from my mind during the writing. So I sit with my pen in hand still contemplating the definition. What could excite such a painstakingly burdensome dream upon me? My cat tells me it's the cheese and how it may have gone bad but I choose to disbelieve that. Nothing has been so enigmatic or educational in my life than my dreams, such bizarre images. A bonanza of stalwart manifestations causes me to over think the simple idea of the dream work and see the craziness that persists to exist in a repressive state. My brain is currently reeling from discovering itself and seeing, in fact remembering, its true potential. A gift that enables it to become more complex. I haven't the foggiest of what the dream was. A mere illusion created by my mind to ease the pain of true discovery? I don't know what else to say about the matter.

3/25/05

Spring has come and the snow remains reminding us of the urgency in which it came. There is a feeling to the knowledge of spring but a different one entirely to being in spring. I discussed with my cat the importance of experiencing spring as oppose to knowing it is spring. He agreed with me, to some extent, implying that knowing and being are equally important. I thought for a moment and considered how I would feel if I knew and experienced spring. It was an ok notion but I favored my own. Experiencing an unknown, joyful feeling is better than having extensive knowledge of it. Without that knowledge you would then wish to know what it is. When someone experiences that feeling they would, or should, start performing a series of tests to answer their question of what they're feeling and why they're feeling this way. Or that person can be simply content in being, a more desirable position in my opinion. My cat said it's stupid for people not to know a season. He then left me hanging in the debate. As a result, I also left the conversation. But something about knowing versus experiencing still frustrated me. Yesterday, I slept hoping to figure it out in my dreams but that was of no use. When I had breakfast this morning, with my waffle and coffee, my cat had his cornflakes in a milk bowl, he revisited the issue. He told me that his argument holds more validity than my own. It is better when someone knows when to plant their crops, wear certain clothes, and/or know that the winter has come to an end. Besides, he added, that eventually a person who knows not of spring will know of it through another name. Knowing of the season and experiencing it are equally important since one will lead into the other. He had a point! Not surprised, though. Most cats derived from a creature called Felonious Catra, an animal who bored their prey to death through explanations of the obvious. That's why cats make good lawyers. But I was too stubborn to admit defeat. So as a course of action I told him that experience is a greater feeling than knowing and I left the room without further discussion. Passive aggression infuriates my cat causing him to wig out. This was my plan. Get him angry enough so that he'll make a mistake in his argument, providing his downfall. As he ran after me I thought about what I was going to say. I forgot what he said or even what I said but I remember eviscerating him verbally. As the day wore on I lorded over him.

Unbeknownst to him that he beat from the very beginning.

6/14/05

As I formatted my disk this morning I realized there is no overcrowded copy room. In any other place scores of people rush in and out wanting something out of that place and yet the copy room is occupied only by one person. It is surprising to realize that people who want their paper do not stay to retrieve it, not even to talk to the copying engineer (the one who sits on the stool and yearns for human contact). In night clubs, people stay for ages and are forced to leave albeit some even find ways of staying, possibly in front or the back of the club. The floppy disk I formatted reminded me of my youth and the 23rd degree I received at college which was a Copying Degree. To some this was the same as a Replication Degree. Though I never did much with it, I still feel pride whenever I tell my friends, my cat, and anyone that would listen that I can operate a copy machine. Why not stay? Nothing bad comes from a copy unless you place the paper in wrong or press the wrong button, or your copying tens of thousands of the wrong item. Whenever I see people I ask how long do they stay at a certain place and they usually shrug or walk faster. The most common answer I get is 'all day' and the most spoken place is 'home'. So people spend more time at their home than a copy room. That seems right. So it is safe to assume that if everyone left their house at the same time and traveled at the same speed then everyone would be at the copy room and finally it would be crowded. Moreover, the copy room clerk or attendant will finally have the company he always wanted. Such a dream is only conjured by me and the copy room clerk/attendant. After thinking about it, I realized my disk can't be formatted because the computer thinks it is broken. Frustrated and too mentally fatigue from the copy room contemplation I decided to eliminate the tiny project. My cat was asleep at this moment so I couldn't ask him to format the disk on his laptop. I had some important documents on this computer and recent power failures made me cautious so I decide to save everything on disk and now I can't because I'm not tech savvy. I could spend my time at the copy room but I have better things to do at home.

I just remembered something I wrote on my computer a while ago. I tried to save it on disk but it didn't work. So I might as well write it down again.

Here it is:

Hey hovering senora,

Many saw you dancing a distance from the window,

Even if you sell kites at a ghetto

Hovering senora, hover on.

Don't be burdened by the tasks you take, rejected and unwanted by the people whom you.

Always smile a blissful smile to all even though you're hated by all.

Don't worry about them, you're loved by me.

So now you can be beautiful without destroying your inner pride

With changes to your bosom and your powerful thighs.

Go forth to the people and be you throughout the hateful cries.

Know you're a senora through and through, an electric girl emancipated.

Forceful yet shy but always a rambunctious youth.

Hovering senora, hovering senora

Hey hovering senora,

Counting sheep atop a tiny hill,

Being whimsical and mischievous,

Through all the pain and suffering,

You acknowledge it without a sound or gesture.

Where were you when I was lost and hated by everyone?

Did you even know about me then or exist?

Hovering senora, hovering senora

That's pretty much what I wrote.

6/05/05

July fourth was a dazzling day. My cat thought of it as another way to hypnotize the masses into being stupid. Me, I just had fun with it. The day began with me waking up and eating a bowl of corn flakes, my cat had a sausage patty. Until the fireworks started, the day was the same as any other, consisting of me walking my cat, playing poker with Pablo's rooster, and watching the news. As I sat watching I noticed that the people who found it necessary to travel hundreds of miles here to watch the fireworks forgot to find a way to occupy the time between 6 a.m. and Midnight. My cat remarked on the gov't's plan to make us stupider every year by blowing up light into the air to decrease our sharpness, not to mention increase the damage to our retinas so as to give optometrists another reason to film contact lens commercials. I never minded his conspiracy theories and decided to sleep until 8 p.m. Soon I woke up, put the leash on my cat and strode off to the bridge to watch the fireworks, the only highlight for July 4th. The walk wasn't as brief as I expected it to be. My cat kept going on and on about how the government wants to control the ignorant populous through pretty colors.

147

Then I proposed my own theory. What about television? My cat thought about this for a while and proceeded on by saying that it was a clever cover-up. He continued noting the chemical compound in common fireworks. The moment we arrived, scores of people were already planting themselves at certain spots for a perfect view of the fireworks. My cat laughed at their idiocy. I, on the other hand, waited in explosive anticipation for the display of lights. As time passed by my Jimmy leg acted up more and more. I guess I couldn't wait for it. Then it happened: brilliant beauty in the guise of bursting supernovas accompanied by the luscious quasar blast. My pupils dilated to intake more and more of the great, miraculous spectacle. I spied my cat taking some fun in the event. Once he saw me watching, he quickly turned away and closed his eyes. I realized that my cat may have been right after all. My ignorance took over. But that's what made it more beautiful, not just the colors or the size of each blast but the whimsy and the energy radiating by the lovers, the families, the children and pets around the place. Sounds stupid yes, but that is what happened. I'd say more about the fireworks but that would be an insane length of paper. After the fireworks ended, my cat and I walked home. While he continued his theories, I wondered if he really noticed that the people weren't getting dumber but rather closer to a true happiness. But then again cats aren't really known for their precision.

9/07/05

I'm seeing more skirts then usual now. It must be college year again. The vulgarity, the stupidity, the comradery, and, best not to forget, the mundane ideas that are worth crap are given at a daily basis by both students and teachers. What does that have to do with an old man like myself, nothing, except they won't get off my lawn! Those damn bastard kids and their rock and/or roll blasting at six in the evening, it's horrific. My cat doesn't mind however, he loves the children. I say, fuck the children. What have they done for me lately? But that was yesterday's attitude, now, today, I feel for them. Truthfully, I believe they don't really know what the hell to do with themselves. If the world were any bigger they would probably kill themselves. The world is already uncertain enough. I'm glad I passed those classes with flying colors. Every time I speak of school and address him on it, my cat tends to stray away from the subject. I think he's sensitive on some past issues. My days at college were of something…, well it was something. Now that I think of it I can't remember much of it. Well that stinks. Here I am writing a diary entry on something actually important and I can't remember.

And I don't want to finish writing early... what should I write then... yesterday, I should write about yesterday... I can' remember it too well... Oh yes! My birthday passed, 09/05/1816, I should write about that... Damn, nothing happened on my birthday... I just asked my cat what I should write about and he said write about what I feel... I think by looking back at the previous words it's apparent that I'm confused and scared. So I guess I can write about confusion and fear. Wait, that's it... College people are confused and scared, all the time. That is what I can talk about, good thinking cat! Subconsciously college people fear everything around them due to the fact that their current surroundings are foreign. Moreover, everything needs to be explained to them. It's good to have a topic to discuss about in a book. Especially one's diary. I think I'll end it here since I'm forgetting everything today.

9/16/05

Another one of my friends died today. I'm
starting to get used to it. I know my friend died
today because the sky looked peculiar, it was bluer
than it should be. Usually the sky turns different
shades of blue when something happens to me. At
first I didn't notice it till I had to lie down on Billy
the Street. The street was empty, and I get tired
sometimes so I laid down to rest. Looking at the sky,
after figuring out someone died, I started wondering
who. With each name that passed through my mind
different emotions passed through me. I knew many
people so quite a bit of time passed. Soon those
thoughts turned to what color the sky would be
when I died. My favorite color is green, maybe it'll be
that color. Or maybe it would be the opposite of
green. What is the opposite of green? As I pondered
this as a car horn blasted behind me. It was my cat.
He had a rent-a-car for the day because he needed to
pick up a new mattress for me. I got into the car and
told him about the friend who died. He said he read
about it in the obituaries. The friend's name was
Mitch. That was his name. I don't know why I
couldn't remember it before. He was a great guy. His
death was surprising but it happens. You can only

stay sad for so long before it begins to affect your total attitude. As my cat and I drove home, I stared out the window still wondering the opposite of green. Halfway home, I wondered how long my cat had left, hopefully, more time than I have. I forget his age at the moment. An old man like me shouldn't be thinking of death. Instead I should be thinking about lunch. Death is inevitable, lunch is a possibility. Moreover, possibilities are uncertain therefore, if it happens, more thought should be placed upon it. It sounds crude and refutable, but I couldn't think of anything else to say. My cat did his best to console me. He's bad at it, but he tries. I like that. I'm proud of him. I still have no idea what color the sky would be when I die. I know it would be a color I hate though.

10/01/05

Being in a perpetual state of happiness is impossible nowadays. This afternoon I walked 'Isadora's Necklace', a Back Bay area where the stream is only good for reflection, and took notice of the hundred squadron racing down the street. I wondered what sort of emergency had the need for so many cadets. My cat would have loved to see it but he had better things to do. I continued walking, watching the foliage make its gradual change to a different color and I wondered if I needed to be interesting to be properly noticed. Do I need to be witty and insightful forever? That's impossible to come up with a new comment every second. I need to think about what I say. This refers to my comment above since people are what one needs to be happy. But if you need to be interesting to be with people then it is not worth it. —By the way, people who do different things everyday do not live fulfilled lives; they are junkies not getting enough. I know for a fact that humans need to have some sort of routine, in conjunction with various spices of life then a person could be fulfilled but only at that median! If that is the case then how are people getting together? In my perspective, it doesn't make sense.

154

A few days ago I saw my cat with another cat and he was doing his best to court her. I overheard some of their conversation. They were talking about how catnip shouldn't just be medicinal. The girl cat, Kit, talked his ear off on the issue. At this point in time I was listening full on for some inspiration on how to impress chicks, that information could be useful down the line. But he said nothing. When she finally stopped talking she made the remark on how just listening to her made him more interesting, then she left. I was perplexed at this point since women, cat or otherwise, complain about inattentive men and how they should change. My cat's only answer to this comment was an 'o.k.' He then walked away and their relationship, or whatever it was, ended. I guess he was looking for someone to love to hate. By the way I think I lost my point somewhere in this entry, it wasn't a big point but that needed a conclusion. I guess this could be it.

10/31/05

I suddenly had the strangest feeling that I don't belong in this frame. It was peculiar, I woke up, put on my slippers, brushed my teeth and at breakfast. When I list my actions in order it doesn't seem strange but the feeling of loss and alienation from the things you own was apparent. I told my cat about this he shrugged and fell back to sleep. He's still sulking over his breakup with Kit. I went out for a walk. Even outside I felt strange and isolated from the world. I felt as if I should be in the future where the theories/concepts of today resemble tomorrow's way of life but with a more advanced look. I hate to use the word 'advanced' but it's all I can really think of at the moment. When one says advanced I immediately think of robots. Anyway, this is how I felt and I don't know why. When I sat down to think someone called my name. It was the woman whom I had sex with in the supermarket. She was a woman now, before she was a lady. We greeted each other and I told her about my predicament. She said maybe I belong in the past. Then I would be bored, if that was the case. I told her that I was uncomfortable here in this time; everything is very tolerable and weird. She then

made a remark that got me thinking, she told me
that it is not the time, but the things I did in that
time frame. I guess I'll just end it here.

6/18/06

It's been too long since I had sex. My last escapade was with the woman at the grocery store, which was too long ago. My cat hasn't had sex either but he has an excuse: he hasn't gone outside in almost 40 days. This is part of his new religion or something, I zoned out while he was talking to me about it. My situation is crueler. I have gone outside and I did talk to people, mostly and nothing. Maybe it's not so bad. I could use the extra energy to make a mech or engineer robotic parts. Both are very interesting subjects. For now, I'll just stew with my juices flowing... that don't sound right. For 15 minutes my cat has been upside-down meditating by rushing blood to his head. I'm proud of his tenacity. I'm letting something like reproduction get in the way of my thinking while my cat hangs like a bat and does all these rituals for a belief he has no proof of. I'm still pissed I haven't had sex. Best way to avoid any mishap is to not think about it... Or perhaps masturbate furiously until my head explodes. It's a waste of my life but it's been too long. Maybe I'm thinking this way because I don't have a steady religion like my cat does. I've lived without discipline most of my life and that is why temptation wins, sometimes. I guess I don't have a steady religion because none suit me well. I like Mechanism but it involves turning yourself into a robot after building a mech. I would definitely join Darwinism if it wasn't too machismo for its own talk about survival of the fittest. I have a big problem with people telling me how fit they are and that their muscles give them the right to my stuff. Cannonism, I'm allergic to gun powder; Born Again Christianity, I have yet to finish the first life I'm living. Game Theorism, my only theory is to buy both Boardwalk and Mediterranean Avenue. Any other religion I think of just has another problem I can't deal with. I think my cat does Yoga; he's been in weird positions all day. I think I'll just tough it out for the sex thing.

6/26/06

My cat and I had an argument about the validity of love in today's age. It all started at the breakfast table where I had my big plate of waffles and butter and my cat had his usual ground meat and eggs. My cat had a dream about his ex-girlfriend and that is what started the argument. He stated love exists within two people as they share themselves exclusively to each other and the world. The dream reminded him of this idea. I immediately retorted with the scientific fact that 'love' is an addiction; the same chemicals are activated in the brain for love as it would for crack or cocaine or heroin or insert random drug here. I ended with the statement, 'love is when you favor another over everyone else, not when you found The One.' This is when he got angry. Ground beef fell out of his mouth and his eyes went bloodshot. He immediately fired back with how scientific approaches don't explain everything. I kindly stated that his response was highly emotional. I then washed our plates and continued the conversation. I stated if science didn't explain everything then everything would be a miracle just like love. He then said something about his experiences with women and how it wasn't an addiction. I reminded him of his catnip problem. He told me he didn't have a problem. He continued with a burning question, if I ever loved someone? For several hours I thought of an answer. Finally I said, no. Out of all the women I courted none of them lived up to expectations. He then asked me what I wanted in a woman. I told him that a woman needed to love me when I had nothing and love me still when I lose everything. Moreover, they only wanted me so they could have a family, not us having a family. My cat looked at me for a while then shook his head. He proclaimed that one day I'll find my own person to be addicted to and I told him to shut the fuck up. Since that argument we haven't spoken to each other. We passed each other in the kitchen and we passed each other in the bathroom. Finally I said something, I forgot what I said, but it got us talking again.

8/06/06

I had a dream last night; I told my cat about it but he couldn't figure out what it means. The boy has a psychology degree and he can't even interpret a simple dream. I wouldn't say 'simple' now that I think about it. Here it is:

In a wasteland, some guy flew up in the sky and watched me buried in pain and dirt. He then stood there, stifling an uproarious laugh, charging a ball of chi in intermediate spurts. By the end of the charge, the ball of energy was a massive Pluto size, hovering above his hand. There was nothing I could do. Just before he let the ball drop, he spoke rather oddly, indecipherable but in a comprehensive language. Then it hit me. Then I woke up.

I've been thinking about it all day, what the scene, the player, and the ball meant. Or rather what they don't mean. After all a cigar could be just a cigar. After a day of constant thinking I finally came up with what this dream could mean. The wasteland was the beautiful landscape of the life I once had. In an instant, it became a desolate field; this was due to inactivity in my life, which is represented by me being in pain. A candid life goes noticed with good memories in hand however my life, younger life, was unmoving. Next is the ball of energy. One could say my regret came back tenfold. Or maybe it's just my life flashing before me in a brilliant fury. Or, lastly, it's just a device for killing me. I don't know what to make of the man. His face seemed ordinary, in fact too ordinary. It forced me to focus on the other body parts that presented no fantastic attributes, but the face was oh so plain. Or perhaps, the man was some form of my younger self. And he wanted to destroy me. I was particularly ordinary in my younger days. I didn't tell that part to my cat but would he have said anything useful. No. I need more time to think about this dream and the gravity of what it means.

8/15/06

My cat and I went to find the hyperbolic time chamber. I went there when I felt like a kid. I was actually in my twenties but I was a kid compared to now. On our way there, my cat met up with his penguin friend, I forget his name at the present moment, and they caught up on old times and prepared for future times. He was on his 10 year tenure at a college; he quit his job at the Ice Cube Company as their lawyer. He said the fight wasn't in his heart anymore. As we walked down the street, past the Cineplex, cutting across Periwinkle quad, down and out of the Communal Zen Garden, we stopped for a quick bite to eat at Cheese Burger Meister Furher. After our meal, five more miles later, we finally arrived at the time chamber. I told the two about my training, realizations, and the virtual space inside. This was before I got my cat so he knew nothing about the experience only that the door to the chamber locks every so often. Only on random trips can one be lucky enough to enter. His penguin friend, Harry (I finally remembered his name!) asked me something I never considered, why did I go? That was something which took me by surprise but only took me a few moments to conjure an answer. But the answer still didn't suffice for me. I spoke about myself, the persona, and our time together in the chamber. I went in to because of a sense of loss from my marriage, the lack of job, and the state of the world at that time. Nothing seemed to work out and I estimated it was due to me. So I left the world. I left the dimension. I left myself. To be what I desired. The persona was for company, for a challenge. After training, I left the chamber and the persona (I think). I still investigate which one of us really left from time to time. After my story, we walked back home and Harry stayed for dinner. We ate spinach and various fish. During the dinner I remembered how I remember little of my younger days. I failed to keep a diary like I do now, but I marked that event as important in my life and had no concrete reason for not recording any future act. Then I thought what else have I missed, or forgotten, of my earlier intentions. Perhaps I can sleep on it. After dinner, my cat's friend went back to the University and I strode back to the chamber. I stared at the now locked door for what seemed like hours.

9/07/06

There was a point in my life when I knew what love was. Eighty years ago my then wife helped me make a startling discovery. Throughout the marriage there have been ups and downs, lefts and rights, and the occasional diagonal; but on few occasions there have been moments where I was there for her. That was when I made an extra addition to the definition. I was never completely there for her and she never allowed me to be. She was the kind of woman to drift on a life raft and refuse help from passing ships because she believed she could paddle herself to safety. She married me to prove some feminist point that flew over my head back then because I was too much in 'love'. My cat looks at me strange every time I explain it to him. Apparently a piece of the definition involves dependence; she was so strong that she supported her own pressures and gravity. I used multiple crutches. There was little sympathy and an abundance of ridicule and criticism. At that point in time, I could tolerate such emotionless sex and speech from her. Now I barely have patience for a rude waiter. Why did she refuse me to be at her side? There were times I wondered that and found no real answer. She never asked of anything from me, getting all she needs from herself. I did not understand what she saw in me or why she stayed till the end of her life. The anniversary is tomorrow and every year I remember a little bit more about the marriage and how it tore me apart. I recovered, gradually. When I got my cat, my days got a little bit better. Now I can say that I'm happy. On days like this, however, I can't help but ponder yesteryears of cold shoulders and absolute misery. Truthfully, I don't know what love is and I can proudly say I never will. Perhaps something interesting will get my mind off of this.

3/1/15

I saw the news in the sky during my radio program, 'The Magnanimous Space Adventures of Ahab & Queequeg'. The sky was magenta. My young daughter passed away. It wasn't swift nor slow, just a simple letting go of her mortality. Something we all hold onto with too much grip. The news came from the mouth of my cat. He immediately slinked away after reciting the doctor's message. I turned off my radio and went for a walk. After 17 miles, I was closing in on the park that my young daughter and I played in. I got used to death some time ago, or was it a long time ago? No matter. I reconciled with the death of friends, but the death of a daughter is different. With friends, your world gets smaller, but remains intact. With your children, your world begins to dim. No matter how large or small it looks uninviting, like a stranger's home outfitted with locks and barred windows. It makes you want to leave. I sat there, on the bench near the fountain, and looked around. It was dusk. The runners and wanderers lessened in number with each minute. Soon there was only myself and one other. He was slumped under a tree, unmoving and peaceful. I suspect him to be sleeping, if not perhaps he's dead too. I wouldn't be surprised that no one noticed or even if they did, no help was given or concern showed. It's what happens when the world becomes faster. Our minds take a long while to evolve but our bodies race to the next major event. Which is a shame, but it's the way of real growth. Slow and calculated. I think I'm just babbling. As I sat there, I'm reminded of today's radio episode. Queequeg was sitting upon an asteroid waiting for Ahab to arrive with their ship, 'The Ivory Tail'. He was looking upon the stars that appeared to zoom. He sighed then recited a poem for his son:

'We walk together in the rain my son

Your tiny hand clasping mine

The drips staining my collar are not from the rain

They are my tears.

They fall for you as we walk together,

Towards the same tree that other fathers and sons go.

They fall because of the future

Where we walk yet stumble like fools

169

They fall because you will be gone soon.

Towards the great future, where you will grow

Where you too will have a son that will grab your hand

With all of his little might

You will go, I will stay. Goodbye.'

I was never able to hold her hand, even when she was younger. I will still cry, at least. That is the best I can do.

5/3/15

The other day, I took my cat out for a walk across the expansion lake near the shack. We came upon a cemetery of the great showmen and showwomen of the past century. Each headstone contained unique epitaphs, short in description, long in depth, on the most tremendous part of their life. My cat strolled around then had a chat with the bug groundskeeper about the area. Ever since the past funeral, he's been persnickety on the care of cemetery lots and gravestones. The groundskeeper, a stick bug I think, kept reaffirming the groundskeeper code and how things are always kept just right. I wandered off to the larger, grander tombstones wondering what sort of feats the goliaths of life performed that warranted cathedrals. Apparently, there was Lenny who read every book ever man wrote and wrote his own compendium for the everyday business man. I read the book. It was 250 pages of succinct trite; a true telling of human imagination. Then there was Abigail, who found ways of curing every disease and created their substitutes so the pharmaceutical market didn't go under. She's the reason Cancer II was an easily treatable disease. In the far corner of the gravesite, there lay Thomas. His headstone was pretty gaudy in that old-school Egyptian way. Towering at 250 ft., lacquered in Onyx, with a hand chiseled inscription of his great work. Thomas performed a feat that all men dared, but he failed spectacularly at. His inscription read:

Here beneath the great sky,

A man no sight wishes to behold.

He followed paths unformed only to walk toward oblivion.

Here within the great earth,

A man whose depth stops nigh of a few yards

An uninteresting specimen

Here, and yet nowhere, is the anti-spirit of humanity.

A striver of needs but no wants, A lover of the plain, a ghost in both life and death...

The inscription went on but I got bored and walked back toward the entrance to wait for my cat. He was still questioning the groundskeeper. To think that these people are important is strange. So